HITLER'S MISTAKES

BY THE SAME AUTHOR

Rommel as Military Commander
Montgomery as Military Commander
Churchill as Warlord
Man of Armour: The Biography of Lieutenant-General Vyvyan Pope
Slim the Standard-bearer: The Biography of Field-Marshal the Viscount Slim
The Life and Death of the Afrika Korps
Ultra Goes to War
The Chief: Field-Marshal Lord Wavell, Commander-in-Chief and Viceroy, 1939–47
The Other Ultra
Freedom's Battle: The War on Land 1939–45 (Ed.)

HITLER'S MISTAKES

RONALD LEWIN

Political misjudgements and wrong turns are like tuberculosis, hard to detect and easy to cure in the beginning and easy to diagnose and very hard to cure at the end.

—NICCOLO MACHIAVELLI

William Morrow and Company, Inc.
New York

First published in 1984 in Great Britain by Leo Cooper in association with Martin Secker & Warburg Limited.

Library of Congress Cataloging-in-Publication Data

Lewin, Ronald.
Hitler's mistakes.

Bibliography: p.
Includes index.
1. Germany--Politics and government--1933-1945.
2. World War, 1939-1945. 3. Hitler, Adolf, 1889-1945.
4. Errors. I. Title.
DD256.5.L5 1986 943.086 85-13757
ISBN 0-688-05821-3

Printed in the United States of America

First U.S. Edition

1 2 3 4 5 6 7 8 9 10

BOOK DESIGN BY RICHARD ORIOLO

To
my dear friend
Dame Lilo Milchsack, CMG,
creator of
The Königswinter Conference
remembering our first meeting
in 1945

CONTENTS

HITLER'S MISTAKES

INTRODUCTION

I first met Ronald Lewin in the early 1970s. He came to New Orleans to talk about Ike, and we talked nonstop for two days. Over the next decade, he came often, staying at my home, giving guest lectures to my students, enjoying the restaurants of New Orleans, but primarily talking history.

During one of his early visits, I took Ronald to the site of the Battle of New Orleans. We tramped over the battlefield as I pointed out General Jackson's position, and the British line of march, and the terrain features. Finally we went to the museum, where Ronald stood transfixed before a display of the regimental badges of the British units involved in the battle, everyone of whom had suffered horrendous losses. Tears streamed down his face. "These are some of our very best regiments," he explained to me. "Those poor men." Wow, I thought, here is a man with a really strong historical sense.

Ronald Lewin was born to be a historian, but it wasn't until relatively late in his life that he found that out. During World War II he was an artillery officer, fighting with Monty across the desert of North Africa, up into Sicily and Italy, then on to Normandy, across France, over the Rhine, the whole way. After demobilization, he joined BBC, where he did very well indeed, rising to Director of the Home Services. Finally, in retirement, he took up the writing of history. He produced first-class volumes on Churchill, Rommel, Slim, and others. The outpouring was climaxed with *Ultra Goes to War,* now universally regarded as one of the classic books on the war, a member of that small handful that will be read—with profit—a hundred years from now.

For all my admiration for Ronald as a historian, however, I'm glad to say that I spent most of my time with him in serious and sustained argument. Glad because he was the most wonderful man to hold a debate with—he knew what he was talking about, he was prepared to listen to and always offered new information, and he was good-humored.

Arguing with Ronald was especially stimulating because he had strong prejudices, which he denied—his opinions, he claimed, were simply rational conclusions arrived at by a process of rational thought. Chief among these conclusions was that, in every strategic disagreement during the war, Churchill and the British were right, Eisenhower and the Americans wrong. Since my prejudices are just the opposite, I was always ready to do battle with him, especially because we were both fully committed to the cause of Anglo-American unity.

During one of his visits to New Orleans, we went to the Naval Reserve Officers Club, where we gave a talk on the strategy of World War II. To the delight of the officers, we got into a heated dispute over the question of a 1943 cross-Channel attack, which Eisenhower and Marshall advocated but which Churchill and the British scuttled, in favor of operations in North Africa. Ronald insisted that a '43 invasion was quite impossible, while I insisted that it could have worked. We hurled facts and opinions at each other, and of course neither one of us moved an inch in our positions.

It was during that visit that I learned how good a soldier Ronald was. My wife, Moira, and I took him out in our canoe for a daylong paddle in Honey Island Swamp, just northeast of New Orleans. It is a vast Deep South swamp, complete with Spanish moss, cypress stands, ibis and egrets, 'gators and snakes. Bayous run off in every direction, one seldom sees the sky, and getting lost is always a danger (the first two dozen times we went, Moira and I always took a topographical map, and colored ribbons to attach to trees to mark our way out). We have taken many friends into Honey Island; always, when we get deep into the interior of the swamp, I ask if our friends can guide us out. None ever has, except Ronald. He had noticed the few landmarks, mainly tall cypress trees, and unhesitatingly told us where to turn at each junction, with the confidence of a soldier who has studied the terrain.

In 1980 I began leading an annual tour of World War II battlefields. Ronald was one of the principal speakers, and the most popular. He was very British, in his manner, his dress, his speech, and his habits, the type that usually irritates Americans. But he got on well with American tourists, even though he delighted in destroying their myths, downplaying Patton and overplaying Monty, deliberately stirring up the group, but withal teaching every minute, forcing the Americans to examine their assumptions and broaden their views.

He would give it to his fellow countrymen as quickly as he gave it to the Americans. On one of my tours, A.J.P. Taylor was the speaker at the opening banquet, at the Savile Club in London. Taylor's theme was the war in the Med, which he pronounced a strategic blunder of the first magnitude. According to Taylor, the Allies never should have fought there at all. When Taylor finished, Ronald announced his verdict, loudly: "I don't agree with a word he said."

Through the years, Ronald and I exchanged discoveries and information. He was exceedingly generous in passing on his finds in various archives. He would call me on the telephone, full of excitement, to tell me that I absolutely had to come to Washington to see this or that documentary collection.

The last time I saw Ronald was at Christmas season, 1983. Moira and I were in England doing research, and spent a weekend with the Lewins at their home in East Horsley. Ronald had a cancer, and the outlook was not good, and he was in pain. Movement was difficult, he knew the end was near, but his spirit still soared. We went up to his study for sherry before dinner. The study was a scholar's dream—bookcases all around, jammed with books. A huge table dominated the middle of the large room. The table space was piled high with books, each one open, all underlined with marginal comments. The typewriter had the place of honor, at the center of everything. Ronald was writing a history of World War II for Oxford University Press, and was about one third of the way through it. We talked about the work, and about the manuscript he had just completed on Hitler's mistakes. He was excited about both books, thought they would have an impact, expected them to do well.

The following morning, we had coffee in his study. Ronald had lost a lot of weight and seemed almost shrunken as he sat, in his bathrobe, gesturing with his unlit pipe. I made the mistake of referring to a "creeping barrage," and he gave me an indignant lecture on proper artillerymen's jargon.* It was Ronald as I will always remember him, teaching, his eyes flashing, passing on information, making his contribution to the writing of better history, most of all—and most inspiring of all— insisting on accuracy of fact and spirit in all historical writing.

* A barrage is a bombardment that moves forward ahead of advancing troops; therefore, "creeping barrage" is redundant.

He died shortly thereafter. He died almost literally at his typewriter; like the good soldier dying with his boots on, he was facing to the front, doing his duty.

On reading *Hitler's Mistakes* some nine months later, I missed Ronald even more than I had already, because there are all sorts of interpretations in the book about which I would love to argue with him. For instance, I'd want to ask, "How come, if Hitler made so many mistakes, he came so close to winning?"

I can just imagine Ronald sticking his pipe in his mouth, his eyes sparkling, the hint of a grin at the corners of his lips. And he might say, "But my dear Steve, the book isn't about the Allies' mistakes. Would you like me to start listing *them*?"

I would indeed. Whatever Ronald had to say about the war was always fascinating and fresh. *Hitler's Mistakes* is that and more. I think myself that the first chapter, on the emptiness at the core of Hitler's being, is as good a use of psychohistory as I have seen, brilliantly applied to Hitler. In *Ultra Goes to War,* Ronald Lewin showed himself to be a master at presenting new information; in *Hitler's Mistakes,* he shows himself to be a master at new interpretations and insights while working from well-known material. The result is a thought-provoking book that has the great added advantage of being a joy to read.

—Stephen E. Ambrose

Eisenhowerplatz
New Orleans, Louisiana
December 11, 1984

1

THE GRANITE BASE

We live as we dream—alone.

—JOSEF CONRAD, *Heart of Darkness*

Side by side with the politician there is a ghostly Nobody, one for whom no other person exists in his own right.

—J. P. STERN, *Hitler: The Führer and the People*

Both Hitler and Jesus of Nazareth were born in an inn. Bizarre though the conjunction may seem, it would probably not have displeased the Führer, in spite of his rancid contempt for the Christian faith. He saw himself in messianic terms. In a speech at Wurzburg in 1937, for example, he announced:

> However weak the individual may be when compared with the omnipotence and will of Providence, yet at the moment when he acts as Providence would have him act he becomes immeasurably strong. Then there streams down upon him that force which has marked all greatness in the world's history. And when I look back only on the five years which lie behind us, then I

feel that I am justified in saying: That has not been the work of man alone.

"There was a man sent from God." *Mutatis mutandis,* the claim is similar.* Even Hitler's opponents were conscious of it. As early as 1924, during the trial that followed the Nazis' abortive *Bürgerbräe Keller Putsch* in Munich, the hostile Bavarian Army commander, General Lossow, testified in the witness box about Hitler's ambitions. "He thought himself the German Mussolini or the German Gambetta, and his followers, who had entered on the heritage of the Byzantine monarchy, regarded him as the German Messiah."

But the conjunction has another relevance. More than all the other despots of history, Hitler has been presented as the supreme personification of a phenomenon which Christian apologetics have struggled for centuries to explain—and to explain away: that inner contradiction within the creed, enigmatic, unresolved, the worm at the heart of the rose. This is, of course, the problem of Evil. It is indeed difficult to correlate the behavior of the man born at Braunau on the Inn with the message and promise of the man born in a manger. Hitler's absolute nihilism, his sadism, his treachery, his mercilessly impersonal indifference to the human race have seemed to represent in so quintessential a form the working of the principle of Evil that many of his critics have been obsessed by it, casting their judgments in moral categories and seeking desperately to find, in some abnormal twist of Hitler's personality, an explanation that can account for a monster. But the moral approach can be overdone. It can, indeed, induce an excess of righteousness which warps the critical faculty. Even Lord Bullock, outstanding among Hitler's biographers, ends by enlarging on "so repellent and so barren a figure" and then declaring that "Hitler will have his place in history, but it will be alongside Attila the Hun, the barbarian King who was surnamed, not 'The Great,' but 'The Scourge of God,' and who boasted 'in a saying,' Gibbon writes, 'worthy of his ferocious pride, that the grass never grew on the spot where his horse had stood.' " Repellent and barren, yes: but not merely an Attila. The frame of reference is absurdly too narrow. "Standing aghast is

* E.g., in *Mein Kampf:* "I believe today that I am acting in the sense of the Almighty Creator: by warding off the Jews, I am fighting for the Lord's work." Or in his speech of December 11, 1942, in which he declared war on the USA.: "A historical revision on a unique scale has been imposed on us by the Creator."

an unrewarding posture for anyone trying to pay close attention to the thread of history." *

It may be useful, therefore, to consider Hitler's career objectively, without the deforming intrusion of moral judgments, to evaluate purely pragmatically the ends at which he aimed and the means that he employed. There is, in fact, a visible consistency of aim. Only the methods alter. In *Mein Kampf* he wrote of his early manhood: "During these years in Vienna a view of life and a definite outlook on the world took shape in my mind. These became the granite basis of my conduct. Since then I have extended that foundation very little. I have changed nothing in it." Untrue: yet the changes in that conception of the world were, in fact, marginal until the day when he lay in the Berlin bunker, shot through the mouth, with Eva Braun dead at his side. Since the teleology of his world view was so stable, Hitler's long-term aims are readily identifiable and therefore the first question is, were they realistic? Whether or not they were attainable, the second question is equally practical: accepting Hitler on his own valuation, did he choose the best methods to achieve those ultimate objectives from which, once he had determined early in life to reach them, his eyes never deviated? There is much to be said for making such an assessment clinically, without the super-heating that tends, in Hitler's case anyway, to be the by-product of moral judgment.

This is immediately evident as soon as one asks oneself, is it possible to apply to Hitler the mordant phrase coined by Tacitus to summarize the career of the Roman Emperor Galba, *omnium consensu capax imperii nisi imperasset*—"Had he never been emperor, no one would have doubted his ability to reign"? For if it could be argued that Hitler's mistakes were merely tactical or strategical, if one could say definitely that his downfall was due simply to errors of judgment committed during the years of supreme dictatorial power, this would still leave the residual implication that in some intelligible sense he was, nevertheless, *capax imperii:* that he was inherently capable of laying the foundations for a *Reich* that would "last a thousand years," that he was *papabile,* a man whose inner nature was such that it would have been perfectly possible for him to establish a durable empire—if only things had not gone wrong. We would then be accounting for his cataclysmic failure in terms of contingent and presumably avoidable

* Franklin L. Ford, introduction to Eberhard Jäckel, *Hitler's World View* (Harvard University Press, 1981); first published in 1969 as *Hitler's Weltanschauung, Entwurf einer Herrschaft.*

error, with the presumption that fundamentally he was a figure like Mahomet who indeed had it in him to create, if not an empire, at least an ambience that would retain a millennial vitality—but that he fumbled his chances. Before the court of history, however, such a plea in mitigation is unacceptable.

For one has to remember that, after all, Hitler was only a human being. During the Second World War and its aftermath, as a result, partly, of Churchillian rhetoric, partly of Allied propaganda and partly of the attempt by postwar German historians to allay their sense of guilt by reaching out for irrational explanations, his image was so magnified that he seemed to many a figure outside the ordinary categories, half shaman, half devil, a sort of supernatural fiend whose very name could frighten children as the looming menace of Napoleon had terrified the young of southern England.* "Be good or Napoleon/Hitler will get you" was a threat that carried awesome implications. But in latter decades the work of demythologizing has been effectively completed. From the evidence of contemporaries, from a plethora of documents, from memoirs and interrogations a Hitler emerges whose feet of clay are so prominent, whose fallibility is so confirmed that it requires a vigorous effort of the imagination to recapture the sense of impotent terror which his name could once arouse. He has been cut down to size, and the scale is human. We can study him now like the objects of W. H. Auden's love poem:

> . . . in my arms till break of day
> Let the living creature lie,
> Mortal, guilty . . .

So we must hold the living Hitler in our imagination—guilty, without a doubt, but no more than mortal. For a historian it is vital to establish the correct universe of discourse, and in considering Hitler the first necessary step is to clear one's vision and switch from the fantasies of myth to the more mundane realm of reality. We no longer need to indulge in demonology.

Once we start to think of Hitler as just another member of the human race we see instantly that what he did derived from what he was: that

* *Gröfaz,* "a name ugly enough to have served some monster of mythology, some twisted Kobbold or goblin embodying and spreading evil" (Craig, *Germany 1936–1945*). But it was merely an abbreviation of *Größter Feldherr aller Zeiten,* the Greatest Warlord of All Times—Keitel's christening of Hitler in June, 1940.

the world view which generated his long-term aims was itself a by-product of his own *persona*—perhaps, in Jungian terms, of his Id. An analysis of Hitler's mistakes must therefore start, in the psychologists' sense, with an analysis in depth. For Hitler, without doubt, must be judged as not *capax imperii,* precisely not capable of creating and bequeathing a Thousand Year Reich, because of the limitations of his own personality. From this inadequate source everything else flowed.* The fact may be presented symbolically. As one thinks of the appalling sufferings of his troops on the Russian front (not to speak of the sufferings of the Russians themselves) one recalls Walter de la Mare's lapidary verdict on Napoleon in 1812:

> What is the world, O soldiers?
> It is I.
> I, this incessant snow,
> This northern sky.
> Soldiers, this solitude
> Through which we go
> Is I.

It is I. Of all the basic traits in Hitler's character—and they are not all that many, in spite of the millions of words that have been written in efforts to diagnose subtle complications—the most notable is his imperious egocentricity and what, we may reasonably ask, is so extraordinary about that? Certainly there is nothing remarkable about the character trait itself. Egocentricity and even egomania are qualities which, whether fruitful or malign in their effects, are shared very generally by artists and murderers, politicians, explorers, soldiers and scientists, including that statistically average unit, the man in the street. Hitler's self-absorption had nothing about it of the demonic, the surreal or the supernatural: it was human and not unusual in its essence. What distinguished it from the concentration on self of a Proust or a Churchill, a Balzac or a MacArthur was its lack of qualification, its nakedness, its totality.

The consequences were certainly grave. It ossified a world view whose objectives, as will be seen, had more shadow than substance

* Thomas Mann put it well in his diary for September 8, 1933: "A man who confounds his hysteria with artistic sensibility, his inner confusion with deep thinking, and without the least doubt or compunction undertakes to impose upon a people with an intellectual tradition as great as Germany's his own thick-headed opinions."

and caused a ruinous misjudgment of the means whereby the unattainable might at least be attempted. Nevertheless, we shall do better to consider the dominating factor in the life pattern of the young Viennese drifter, the former runner on the western front, who had won, in four years, the Iron Cross but no more than a corporal's stripes, as a commonplace phenomenon which in Hitler's case happened to take an extreme form. Extreme indeed, in that suicide is the egoist's final sanction, the admission to himself and to the world that reality has proved stronger than his dreams. On more than one occasion when he looked like being thwarted Hitler threatened suicide and finally, when his ego had no escape route left, selected it as the least unsatisfactory option. Demons, on the whole, are made of tougher metal.

> What though the field be lost?
> All is not lost; the unconquerable will,
> And study of revenge, immortal hate,
> And courage never to submit or yield:
> And what is else not to be overcome?

Hitler would have made a poor showing in *Paradise Lost*.

For long after 1945 it was fashionable, particularly in Germany (though A.J.P. Taylor provides a notorious British example), to maintain that Hitler lacked anything like a world view, if only in the strictly practical sense that, even though he claimed that he acted with "the certainty of a sleep-walker," his operations, whether political or military, were undertaken without any formal basis of clearly perceived principles. On this view his *Kampf* was merely a *guerre de course,* a running fight conducted *ad hoc* without any definitive objectives. But the idea that Hitler was merely an inspired opportunist is void. The mountain of contemporary documentation is now so high that nobody prepared to mine its rich deposits can argue otherwise. Without engaging in the scholiasts' controversy about the precise month or year in which the light dawned on Hitler, one can assert positively that well before he grasped supreme power in 1933—and that itself, on his own confession, had long been his aim—all his activities were directed, and thereafter continued to be directed, toward two main ends. These were the unification (and ultimate expansion) of the Greater German *Volk*—primarily by reversing the intolerable consequences of Versailles—and the elimination of "international Jewry." Though they may have sprouted as the hectic dreams of a down-and-out resentfully absorbing the nationalist tracts and slogans of postwar Munich, they were systematized into an order which is logical and structured. A historian is not concerned with magnanimity, but with truth: still, it would be less than magnanimous, just as it would be incorrect, to deny to Hitler the one intellectual achievement in which he took pride, the core and substance of his own published work, and to insist that his career was a performance without a program, a Wagnerian drama without its *leitmotiv*.

Cynics like Hermann Rauschning have claimed that in its utter nihilism National Socialism, of which Hitler was the paradigm, sought only "a total revolution of all the elements of order," that the acquisition of power was its essential purpose, and that anything else lying in the way was expendable, whether it be professed doctrines of foreign and economic policy or old and loyal campaigners in the struggle. Even anti-Semitism, in Rauschning's view, becomes a means to an end and not an end in itself. Hitler is now no more, in Lord Bullock's words, than "an opportunist without principle."

Can this be true? Or ought we rather to listen to the words of one who suffered but survived, Hans Berndt Gisevius, and who in the introduction to his memoirs *To the Bitter End* wrote that "we must have the intellectual alertness to draw the significant lessons from the downfall of all three German empires of the past: the Hitler dictatorship, the Bismarckian reign, and the Prussia of Frederick the Great"? Gisevius, who said of *Mein Kampf* that "if one reads it carefully, one finds in it everything, literally everything, which this man has brought into the world." When a veteran with this perception equates Hitler's regime with that of Bismarck or Frederick he is certainly not suggesting that the Nazis' Reich was founded, sustained and expanded (even though it was finally destroyed) by a mere opportunistic freebooter who built without a blueprint and traveled without a map. What he is really saying, in effect, is that anyone who believes this has either not read or misread *Mein Kampf*.

Hitler himself was sure where he stood. "The programmatic thinker of a movement," he wrote, "has to determine its goals, the politician has to strive for their attainment. Accordingly, the former is guided in his thinking by eternal truth, the latter's action depends to a greater extent on the practical realities of the moment. The greatness of the former lies in the abstract soundness of his idea, that of the latter rests on the appropriate attitude to the given realities and on their meaningful use, for which the goal of the programmatic thinker has to serve him as his guiding star." Decode this verbiage and the message, issued in 1927 in the second volume of *Mein Kampf,* is crystal clear: "I know exactly where I am going and nothing is going to prevent me getting there." We ought to accept the so-called "programmatic thinker" on his own terms and concentrate on the quality and viability of his program, rather than on attempts to prove that it never existed.

In so doing we are compelled to face, at the outset, an element in Hitler's personality which radically affected his vision of ends that might be achieved and fatally misled him in his choice of means. His egoism was so comprehensive that there was no field in which he could tolerate the possibility of anyone but himself being in absolute control. The judgment of Tacitus on Galba is preceded by another clause—*maior privato visus dum privatus fuit,* "when he was an ordinary citizen he seemed too big for his station." So it was with Hitler. During the years when he was fighting for political power, it is noticeable that it was he who fanatically insisted on precedence. Any self-subordination, whether it be to a Hindenburg, a Papen or a junta of industrialists, was always no more than a calculated and temporary maneuver. After he had gathered all the reins into his hands, his authority was untrammeled and incomparable; for Churchill and Roosevelt were hampered by checks and balances within their respective democratic systems; behind the Japanese warlords there was always the Emperor, and even Stalin, for all his ruthless centralization, never exacted from his officers that oath of loyalty which so disastrously bound the General Staff to the person of their Führer.

This self-centeredness had another facet. Though Hitler thought of himself as an instrument supplied by Providence for the advancement of great causes—and was ready enough to announce the fact to an audience, whether private or public—it somehow happened that whenever difficulties arose the instrument took precedence over the cause: the cause, in fact, had failed Hitler, and never *vice versa*. This is another way of remarking on his inability to contemplate self-sacrifice: suicide as a line of flight, yes, but at no time does one sense in Hitler the spirit of self-abnegation which distinguished so many Germans of his own generation. Of course he did his duty as a front-line soldier; but there can be larger loyalties, and greater sacrifices. Suspended by meat hook and piano wire, those who paid with their lives for participation in the July, 1944, conspiracy and, in the film of their last agony, gave their Führer a voyeur's revenge, represent a capacity to give, and to give at any cost, which was wholly foreign to his nature.

He was a man for whom "I" was more precious than "Idea." From this inversion many of his mistakes derived.

The insulating weakness can be vividly illustrated by his behavior during two of the most critical episodes of his career. Each time, it might be said, he acted more like a rat than a lion. On November 9, 1923, in the closing phase of the Munich *Putsch,* Hitler marched in column through crowded streets toward the Odeonsplatz and the War Ministry where Röhm and his storm troopers were besieged. Though he carried a pistol, Hitler (as he stated during the trial that followed) was in fact confident that the Army would not open fire. Men with names famous or, later, infamous were in his company—Ludendorff, Göring, Rosenberg, Streicher. But shots *were* fired, and sixteen Nazis fell dead. Ludendorff, with his adjutant at his side, continued to march straight to his front. "Not a single man followed him," Alan Bullock wrote. "Hitler at the critical moment had lost his nerve. According to the independent evidence of two eye-witnesses, one of them a National Socialist—Dr. Walther Schultze and Dr. Karl Gebhard—Hitler was the first to scramble to his feet and, stumbling back toward the end of the procession, allowed himself to be pushed by Schultze into a yellow motor-car on the Max Josef Platz. He was undoubtedly in great pain from a dislocated shoulder, and probably believed himself to have been wounded. But there was no denying that under fire the Nazi leaders had broken and fled, Hitler the first."[1] This was not the performance of his troops during the dreadful battle for Stalingrad, whom Hitler was to accuse of craven betrayal, or of the Luftwaffe's fighter pilots whom Göring so wantonly wrote off as cowards, the Gallands, the Steinhoffs.[2] Such men knew that death has no dominion over the dedicated.

Though in the second episode Hitler himself chose death, the impropriety of his action is in no way diminished. The climacteric came on April 22, 1945, when the Russians were already forcing their way into Berlin and Hitler held a long and tempestuous conference. The evidence of those present—Keitel, Jodl, Freytag von Loringhoven and others—is inevitably incoherent, but Hugh Trevor-Roper pieced together the mosaic. "Hitler flew into a rage. He shrieked that he had been deserted; he railed at the Army; he denounced all traitors; he spoke of universal treason, failure, corruption, and lies; and then, exhausted, he declared that the end had come. At last, and for the first time, he despaired of his mission. All was over; the Third Reich was a failure, and its author had nothing left to do but to die."[3] Germany had failed Hitler, not Hitler Germany, so he was prepared in revenge to smash Germany into the dust and then die to avoid the personal degradation of becoming a captive of the USSR. Yet this was the man who had written in *Mein Kampf* that "if a racial entity is being led toward its doom by means of governmental power, then the rebellion of every single member of such a *Volk* is not only a right, but a duty."

How could this be? How could the creator of the Third Reich give orders to Speer during the last days (which Speer of course evaded) to demolish the country's very means of existence, its utility services and communications, its industries, its food supplies? Every locomotive, every goods truck and passenger carriage, every barge or cargo vessel was to be wrecked; every river or canal was to be rendered impassable. "It is best for us to destroy even these things," Hitler told Speer. "For the nation has proved to be the weaker, and the future belongs solely to the stronger nation in the East. In any case only those who are inferior will remain after this struggle, for the good have already been killed." This is the voice of anarchic and self-regardin nihilism, not of the shepherd of his flock, the father and Führer of his people for whom the Cause is greater than the Ego. And no one has identified its source more accurately than Albert Speer. "It sometimes seems to me," he wrote in *Inside the Third Reich,* "that his seizures of violence could come upon him all the more strongly because there were no human emotions in him to oppose them. He simply could not let anyone approach his inner being because that core was lifeless, empty." [4]

This is why any study of Hitler's mistakes, his errors of omission or commission, must be rooted in a proper perception of his personality. *Ex nihilo nihil fit,* runs the old Latin tag: nothing produces nothing. To understand the vacuum at the heart of his "inner being" is to have taken the first essential step toward understanding why all that he did ended in negation. "Though I speak with the tongues of men and of angels, and have not love, I am become as sounding brass, or a tinkling cymbal . . . Love suffereth long, and is kind; love envieth not; love vaunteth not itself, is not puffed up, doth not behave itself unseemly, seeketh not her own; is not easily provoked, thinketh no evil; rejoiceth not in iniquity, but rejoiceth in the truth." All that St. Paul was professing was beyond Hitler's comprehension, and this, perhaps, was the greatest mistake of all.

Shift the focus from the general to the particular, from the nation to the individual; it then becomes painfully and perhaps even poignantly evident that both nature and nurture (to use the language of the Victorian controversy about evolution) denied to Hitler those warm human relationships which, in the case of other great leaders, have enriched their personalities and supplied them with a buttress in their times of tension. So far as can be observed, Hitler never had a friend. Inevitably not, for the intimacy and strength of friendship grow from giving as well as taking. The best that he himself ever claimed was "comradeship," the clinging together of the veterans who had shared his early struggles—his wartime sergeant-major in the List Regiment, Max Amann whom he made the publisher for his Party; second-rate survivors like Ley, Bormann and Hess; Goebbels, Streicher, the photographer Hoffmann. (And even "comradeship" proved to be a frail bond in the end, for Hess defaulted, Himmler turned Judas, and Göring abandoned the sinking ship.) The vapidity of these relationships is depressingly revealed in the *Bormann-Vermerke,* those records of the nightly table talk at his wartime command posts in east Prussia and the Ukraine: table talk, incidentally, which only began long after Stalingrad, when Hitler was plunged into such an abyss of gloom that for months his only mealtime companion was his Alsatian dog. "In the end he settled down to a regular but often bored or uncomprehending audience of his female secretaries, varied occasionally by his hard-drinking, troublemaking adjutant, his quack-doctor, and—after July, 1944, when he was afraid of being poisoned unless he showed her exaggerated attention—his vegetarian-cook." [5] What characterized these curious assemblies was the fact that the "table talk" was never more than a monologue.

How different was this inane and sterile society from that which surrounded Churchill! In peace and in war, at Chartwell, at Chequers and in Downing Street the flow of old and new friends was continuous and the dialogue unrepressed. It was typical of Churchill's magnanimity that "laughter and the love of friends" was the sea in which he swam, that he understood the need to give himself as well as to take from others, and that loyalty in personal relations was his habit and faith. The testimony of those who were admitted to the large and varied circle of intimates, whether it be his private staff or great public figures, is unanimous: once a friend, always a friend—for better or for worse, since it could be guaranteed that if anyone was down on his luck Churchill would be the first to rally to his side. And if the old man from time to time indulged in monologue or soliloquy as much as Hitler, this did not mean that those at his table were deterred from speaking their mind or that argument was not only enjoyed, but encouraged. The important point is that in his conduct of affairs Churchill was refreshed, stimulated and sometimes compelled to adjust his own ideas by living amid what was, in effect, an open society.

Nothing like this happened to Hitler. Yet it was peculiarly necessary for a man of his temperament. The intuitive, of which he was a supreme example, requires the uninhibited criticism of advisers whom he respects and who can warn without fear, for his intuitions may often be wrong. As we examine Hitler's mistakes in detail it will be seen that over and over again they might have been avoided or mitigated if his myopic and suspicious self-assurance had allowed him to listen as well as to dictate. Keitel the "lackey," Jodl, Brauchitsch, Halder and Zeitzler seem like puppets on the end of a string if Hitler's treatment of them be compared with Churchill's symbiotic relationship with his Chiefs of Staff. Is a Nazi equivalent of Alanbrooke's diaries imaginable—diaries which, for all their pages of furious frustration, are the record of fundamental harmony and unstinted admiration for his Prime Minister? Even Roosevelt, who was not on such easy terms with General Marshall, nevertheless held the Chief of Army Staff in such high regard that he denied him the prize of overall command in the Normandy invasion because he simply could not contemplate a life without Marshall's presence in Washington. Hitler, by contrast, reached a point where he could scarcely bring himself to talk to his generals officially, and exiled them from his private circle. This, as they say, is not the way to run an army.

The existence of this loner who lacked the support and consolation of friendship was even more arid in another human dimension: he never knew the full communion of reciprocal love. Mutual love, like friendship, involves a measure of giving, of self-surrender. Whether the relationship be heterosexual or homosexual is in this respect a matter of indifference: Hitler knew neither. Nobody would claim that it is essential for the grand decision-makers and commanders that they should feel themselves to be but a half of a whole, since history is littered with examples to the contrary and, very relevantly, the memoirs of Stalin's daughter Svetlana have revealed a monolith rather than the half of that human arch which we think of as a true marriage.[6] Nevertheless, merely to raise the point is to indicate how, in this regard too, Hitler's life was a barren wilderness. What might have seemed like a flowering—his unwholesome, possessive passion for his niece Geli Raubal—is obscure in many of its details. Her death by shooting in his Munich flat on September 18, 1931, whether occasioned by suicide or some less reputable cause, was certainly shattering in its effect on Hitler, but whatever the character of his feeling for her it has an unnatural tone, there is a probability that it was not reciprocated, and one has but to think of Hitler treating Geli as an equal partner to see that this is incredible. As Queen Victoria preserved her husband's possessions and personal paraphernalia, so Geli's room at the Berghof was kept like a shrine, immaculate and unchanged, but the nature of the implicit loss was utterly different. As for Eva Braun, all she had to offer to Hitler was little more than the servility of a gangster's moll.

Once again, the contrast with Churchill is illuminating. His own assertion that after he married Clementine Hozier he lived happily ever after was no conventional sentimentality: it is demonstrably true, and a mere glance at that lifelong union carries one into a world which Hitler was never able to enter. That world, noticeably, was one of sustained respect between equals. Time after time, as one reads their correspondence, one observes Clemmie advising, reproving, commending, encouraging—frankly, fearlessly and so often wisely. But Hitler "could not let anyone approach his inner being because that core was lifeless, empty." He was a Hollow Man inhabiting a Waste Land.

Nevertheless, the significance of this dead center of his personality must be placed in the right perspective. The lack of friend or lover was an impoverishment for his spirit and left him without mentor, confessor, confidant or comforter. But this private desolation was as nothing compared with the continentwide wilderness which he created in the name of German civilization—created, moreover, because the human being called Adolf Hitler was castrated, incomplete, a eunuch lacking the vital component, humanity. A world view which admits the concept of an inferior species of mankind is radically flawed, but Hitler thought less of mankind in general than he did of his Alsatian dog. At the lifeless and empty core of his inner being all his mistakes had their origin. But we are not looking at a granite base so much as at the dust and ashes on the joyless surface of the moon.

THE CITY OF MAHAGONNY

No Empire intoxicated with the red wine of power and plunder of weaker races has yet lived long in this world.

—MAHATMA GANDHI, *Young India*

What the aristocratic basic idea of Nature desires is the victory of the strong and the annihilation of the weak or his unconditional subjection.

—ADOLF HITLER

History took an ironic turn when Kurt Weill and his librettist Bertolt Brecht presented their opera *The Rise and Fall of the City of Mahagonny* for the first time at Leipzig in March, 1930. It was devised as a satire on the self-indulgent materialism of a moribund Weimar Republic. In retrospect, however, its strident orchestration and the bitter symbolism of its text seem to convey a different meaning. We may see it now as an extraordinary foreshadowing of the fate of Hitler's Germany. It is not surprising that the Leipzig bourgeoisie booed and whistled at a world première which was almost a riot; that after a performance at Berlin's *Kurfürstendamm* in December, 1931, it was to be many years before the opera was revived; or that Nazi propagandists condemned it as a degenerate reflection of cultural bolshevism. They were listening to the voice of Cassandra.

Mahagonny is a dream city on whose portals the Rabelaisian invitation *"Fay ce que vouldras"* might well have been inscribed, a permissive Nirvana where the gross sensuality and materialism which, in Brecht's view, characterized capitalist society could be freely and fully enjoyed. We are never quite sure where it is: in gold-digging California, perhaps—but then it seems to lie beneath the moon of Alabama. Or is it Florida? Today, no doubt, Las Vegas would have been written into the script. As the promoters of this dreamland peddle its seductions among the other cities of the world, people are drawn thither in the hope that the emptiness of their lives may somehow be gilded by glamour: the fantasies of a Hollywood musical now seem within their grasp.

But the bubble bursts. There is discontent, and then disillusion. "This was called Mahagonny, the city of nets, but in the net nothing has been caught." A hurricane threatens. People start looking for a new Paradise somewhere else: God, who appears to have been one of the city's founders, cannot send them to Hell for their transgressions because, they say, "We always were in Hell." As the curtain falls a desperate chorus is heard from the burning ruins: "We can't help ourselves, or you, or anyone." Surely it is 1945, and these are the apocalyptic scenes in Berlin, or Hamburg, or the Ruhr? Indeed, the refrain of Lotte Lenya's famous "Moon of Alabama" number in the opening scene on that first night in 1930, "I tell you, I tell you, I tell you we must die" now seems like a *leitmotiv* that would echo and re-echo hauntingly over the conurbations, the concentration camps and the battlefields of Europe for another fifteen years. Hitler had, in fact, envisaged his own Mahagonny and seduced the German people with its delusive charms. The name he gave to it was The Thousand Year Reich—"but in the net nothing has been caught." Brecht's dream city and Hitler's dream empire were equally pie in the sky.

Of course there are many Hitlers; in particular Hitler the instinctive, Hitler the opportunist, Hitler of the "lightning-quick" "ice-cold" decisions. But there is also the man who wrote of himself in *Mein Kampf:* "It may happen occasionally within long periods of human life that the programmatic thinker and the politician become one." However we may define the concept of "the programmatic thinker," it certainly means a man who is working toward an objective; and it is equally certain that the two main objectives at which Hitler aimed with increasing determination were the laying of foundations for a Thousand Year Reich and the extirpation of "international Jewry."

These are the basic ideas, and it is easy to calculate the necessary priorities. For "international Jewry" is an umbrella phrase under which Hitler compacted at least three disparate groups: the ghetto Jews, primarily of eastern Europe; the "Jewish Bolshevists" who were responsible for all that "November, 1918," meant to Hitler himself, and for the rise of Soviet Russia; and another body, at once less definable, more extensive and more cosmopolitan, the real "international Jewry" which, lurking in the great centers of power abroad, the banks, the industrial complexes and even the governments, pulled the strings and made the world its puppet. Without the conquest of western Europe and, at least, European Russia the first two groups could not be annihilated. Only a world hegemony could settle Hitler's account with the third group.* In simple practical terms, therefore, an attack on his main objective must logically precede (though it might also be accompanied by) the attainment of his second aim. The creation of a Greater Germany capable of expansion into a Thousand Year Reich had necessarily to be the primary purpose of the programmatic thinker. Yet amid all his mistakes this can be identified as the fundamental error.

There are many cartographical problems for anyone who sets out to map the route by which Hitler's mind finally arrived at this grandiose project. Yet the problems become easier once the elusive character of his mind's functioning is properly understood. He was rarely a linear thinker, whose calculations moved from one point to another in the far distance with the certainty and simplicity of a mathematical or a logical demonstration. Men of large scope, the great decision-makers (whether they be a Napoleon, a Churchill, a Roosevelt or a Hitler), are like conjurors who constantly keep a number of options in play. Moreover, not only are they capable of simultaneously carrying in their heads two or more incompatible propositions: even a single idea be-

* At the notorious Wannsee conference in January, 1942, when Heydrich laid down the ground plan for the Final Solution, he warned the representatives from the *Reich*'s various ministries about the danger of allowing the "strongest" of the Jews to survive. These, he said, could become "the germ cell of a new Jewish revival" and must be "appropriately dealt with." The lists submitted by Heydrich at Wannsee actually included figures for the Jews in neutral Sweden, Switzerland, Spain, Turkey, Portugal and southern Ireland. Only ten days later, in his speech at the Sports Palace in Berlin, Hitler declared: "The result of this war will be the complete annihilation of the Jews." A purge such as Hitler and Heydrich had in mind logically entailed world conquest.

comes Protean as, in their brooding, they bend and twist it to discover unrealized possibilities or unexpected flaws. Curiously enough, the way that Hitler's mind worked in this respect, the meandering course by which he ultimately arrived at the dominating idea of a millennial German Empire, is perfectly described in a letter which Beethoven wrote to the violinist Louis Schlosser in an attempt to articulate his own method of composition:

> Once I have grasped a theme I shall not forget it even years later. I change many things, discard others, and try again and again until I am satisfied: then in my head I begin to elaborate the work in its breadth, its narrowness, its height, its depth, and since I am aware what I want to do the underlying idea never deserts me. It rises, it grows, I see and hear the image in front of me from every angle.*

For Hitler, of course, there were two main themes—Greater Germany and the Jews—which he developed in an increasingly elaborate counterpoint. Each was already active in his head before 1914, and long before he seized power we can see them intertwined within a statement which seems to envisage a limitless expansion of Germany's dominions. Certainly it is not without significance that on the very last page of Part Two of *Mein Kampf* (published in December, 1926), he declared: "A state which in this age of racial poisoning dedicates itself to the care of its best racial elements must some day become *the lord of the earth.*"†

Yet the idea did not strike him at first in its totality. In fact a study of its growth illustrates how in this as in all other respects (including the Jews) the "programmatic thinker" did not begin with a ready-made program but rather rationalized, articulated and expanded the gut reactions of his youth into a full-scale project as a result of his own resentful response to the events of his lifetime, the gradual acquisition of power which enabled him to "do something about it," and the final, but in the end fatal, assumption that by the use of threats or force he could "get away with anything." In other words there is a substantial difference between the raw ideas festering in the mind of

* Hitler himself put this very well in some remarks to Rauschning. "No matter what you attempt, if an idea is not yet mature you will not be able to realize it. There is only one thing to do: have patience, wait, try again, wait again. In the subconscious the work goes on. It matures, sometimes it dies. Unless I have the inner, incorruptible conviction: *this is the solution,* I do nothing."

† Author's italics, Speer later confessed that "in his presence we felt we were lords of the universe."

the pre-1914 Viennese Hitler and the purposes of the omnipotent Führer. The one has volitions, but the other has a timetable.

Hitler's initial pan-Germanism was a child of the Hapsburg Empire, and this is not surprising in view of the circumstances of his early years. He was a displaced person of a particular kind—one who turns in bitterness against his home country and devotes himself with excessive passion to the land of his adoption: it is always ironic to think that this Austrian screamed louder on Germany's behalf than any true-born German of his time. The displacement was double. First, the loss of a home. The picture he later presented of maltreatment by his father may be honest, though it may equally have become as necessary for him to promote a fiction as, in his later years, Montgomery was driven by inner compulsions to pretend (far from accurately) that his mother had overshadowed him like some malign Upas tree. In any case, Alois Hitler died in January, 1903, and his wife, Klara, who evidently overindulged Adolf, was killed by cancer in December, 1908. The roots had withered. "With my clothes and linen packed in a valise, and with an indomitable resolution in my heart, I left for Vienna." He never, in any significant sense, had a home again.

The other displacement was more important, if "important" be accepted as a value judgment which ignores the psychological possibility that the tone and structure of Hitler's personality were permanently conditioned during those early days with Alois and Klara. For one does not forget that

> In the lost childhood of Judas
> Christ was betrayed.[1]

Still, it was the shift from an Austrian upbringing to utter commitment as a true German that set him on the road to the Thousand Year Reich. (But he was only three years old, it is worth noting, when his father was posted to the Austrian Custom House at Passau on the Inn—a Custom House which, somewhat unusually, was located on the *Bavarian* side of the frontier. The coincidence was symbolic—for Hitler, at least, who boasted in *Mein Kampf* that "the German of my youth was the dialect of Lower Bavaria; I could neither forget it nor learn the Viennese jargon.")

The real conversion occurred during Hitler's depressed and solitary years in Vienna between 1908 and 1913 (when he left for Munich): the years when he was a frequenter of the rooming house and the cheap café, a casual laborer making a few crowns occasionally by drawing posters or advertisements and peddling his crude paintings. (There is a fascinating recollection of him in 1910, with his hair falling from beneath a greasy black hat over the collar of an old and overlong topcoat, and the eyes in his thin starved face staring out above a black beard—the very image of a Jewish bagman.) But those who dismiss *Mein Kampf* as mere verbal diarrhea should note how acutely this apparent layabout analyzed the objective reality of the Hapsburg Empire.

He saw it, rightly, as a doomed attempt to reconcile the irreconcilable, a mosaic of incompatible races whose cement was already crumbling. He saw the German element, valuable though its contribution might be, refused its proper place in the sun and decisively separated from its blood brothers across the border by the exclusion after Sadowa, in 1866, of the German Austrians from the new German empire toward whose Kaiser Hitler now looked with admiration. Here was a führer! The man had created the German Navy! He saw, too, that the pan-Germanic movement in Austria itself lacked spirit and strength. There was only one possible course. The Germans in Austria must be led or swept back home into the embrace of a truly Germanic unity. The Hapsburgs, and their zoo of nationalities, could go to hell. Intellectually and emotionally, Hitler had not gone far beyond this point when, in October, 1914, he entrained with the Bavarian List Regiment for the First Battle of Ypres.

It was the cataclysmic events of November, 1918, which caused a new conversion, for Germany itself, in whose interests he had now fought as well as thought, had evidently been foully betrayed. Defeat gave him a rationale, and revolution supplied his opportunity. The problem now was not theoretical, but practical: what must be done? Put simply, Hitler spent the twenties working out the steps that must be taken to restore Germany and acquiring the political muscle which would give him the power to act, and the thirties in discovering, action by action, that what was desirable was attainable. This is the period when the concept of a Greater Germany balloons until, well before 1939, in Hitler's thoughts and speeches it has spread out to the dimensions of a Thousand Year Reich.

By the time that he had completed *Mein Kampf* in the mid-twenties he had not only come to see that the method must be to convert Germany from a shilly-shallying democracy into a taut instrument of war under his own dictatorial control, he had already defined the war plan. Keep Britain and Italy neutral, sedate Poland and the Hapsburg remnants, obliterate France so that "all's quiet on the Western front," and then carve an empire, tactfully called "living space," out of Russia. Here is to be the German raj, permanently occupied and pitilessly exploited. "What India was for England the spaces of the East will be for us." The strong are to reduce the weak to unconditional subjection. "This crude Social Darwinism, in which racial groups fought for the land which could provide the means of subsistence . . . was derived from a view of history as deterministic as that of Marx, but substituting race for class as the key to understanding."

The various political and military *Putsches* of the thirties, which culinated in the launching of Operation Barbarossa in the summer of 1941, were all, whether successful or abortive, whether calculated or impulsive, forward moves toward the fulfillment of that idea of a greatly expanded Germany which the programmatic thinker had disclosed years earlier to a world which either ignored, discounted or ridiculed what he had written.

By 1942, as his *Panzers* roll toward the Caucasus, he is beginning to think about India. And for what purpose was he planning even earlier, in the spring of 1941, a vast naval base at Trondheim which, with its shipyards and docks, would ultimately involve a city of 250,000 Germans? Speer is explicit that Hitler had "already made up his mind" about this project and describes how on June 21 he and Raeder had a conference with Hitler in the Chancellery, when he "determined the approximate site of the city."[2] Another immense naval base was to be carved out of Lorient, St. Nazaire and the Channel Islands. These were shadows cast by the future.*

> Further still and further
> Shall thy bounds be set

seems to have applied also to "the Teutonic Empire of the German Nation." Today, Germany. Tomorrow, the world!

We must in fact assume that, if everything had gone as Hitler intended, and Germany had been victorious, the dynamism which char-

* Toward the end of the war the Germans were developing at Peenemünde the A10, a two-stage rocket designed to reach America. (R. V. Jones, *Most Secret War*, p. 463a.) It is also worth noting that in the summer of 1941 German postwar projections included an armada of 25 battleships, 8 aircraft carriers, 50 cruisers, 400 U-boats and 150 destroyers. With Great Britain and Russia theoretically eliminated, the obvious target for this massive force was the United States.

acterized all his activities, the "Excelsior" spirit which drove him ever onward must have made his empire an "expanding universe." Here, then, is the central question. We are not concerned with short-term military conquests, for we know that Hitler overran most of Europe and might even, with more efficient preparation and execution, have defeated Britain in 1940 and/or Russia in 1941. The basic question is concerned with the long term. "A Thousand Year Reich" may be merely an emotive phrase, but it certainly stands for something more than a military occupation, however extended. What Hitler envisaged was a settled and durable empire comparable with those of the past. Why was such an ambition his fundamental mistake?

Hitler was not pursuing a phantom. An empire is obviously not an impossibility, though many factors may determine its duration—external aggression on the one hand, and on the other the interplay within its frontiers of many fissiparous forces, social, political, economic, religious, racial. Yet empires have existed and endured, even to a millennial extent like the Roman and the Islamic, while those like the British, whose life is measured in centuries, have left their indelible mark. The mistake made by Hitler, who took such pride in his study of history, was that he failed to learn anything from the lessons of the past: failed, that is, to identify features common to earlier empires which—apart from the brute force he understood—had contributed to their distinctive vitality.

Whatever the amount of blood shed on the way, whatever the rapine and loss of "human rights" involved, nevertheless successfully dominant nations have brought in their train a number of offerings which have palliated and even improved the lot of those they have conquered. Few empires have flourished which have not, for example, allowed the common man some measure of hope—whether hope of economic improvement or, through retaining his own or adopting an imported religion, the eschatological prospect of a future life. "Hope, the best comfort of our imperfect condition, was not denied to the Roman slave," wrote Gibbon, and there was good reason to support his famous cadenza, "If a man were called to fix the period in the history of the world during which the condition of the human race was most happy and prosperous, he would, without hesitation, name that which elapsed from the death of Domitian to the accession of Commodus." For Gibbon is, in effect, summarizing a vast amount of evidence which shows how, at its best, the Roman Empire exercised a tolerant mastery, under which the peoples of its provinces prospered.

With all its black spots—the Irish, the Boers—this, too, has been the paternalistic record of the British. The work of the young zealots of the Indian Civil Service, or of a Lugard in Africa, speak for themselves. Even the conquistadors of Islam or Spain brought with them, at the very least, a faith which, if adopted by the conquered, proffered an eschatological promise to the least of men. And frequently there is another benefit: the moderating rule of law which characterized the British Empire and suffused the Roman. In the case of Islam, of course, its vitality (though this too often looks like bigotry without compensating qualities) is still visible today.

But to the people whose lands were to form the far-flung Teutonic empire of the German nation, Hitler could offer no more than thralldom or extinction. Such is the message of *Mein Kampf:* the East is the realm of the lesser man. Apart from this ideological myopia, he intentionally eliminated everything that might in any way generate among the conquered even a gleam of hope. National Socialism *per se* (unlike, for example, the possibility of Roman citizenship, the benefits of Pax Britannica or, for that matter, Communism) had nothing to proffer to those outside the pale. Not once, moreover, does Hitler suggest the possibility of economic advancement for anyone but his own. The Romans took their gods abroad and domesticated them: with the British and the Spanish (even though the Inquisition came too) went Christianity and the chance of being born again. The Islamic faith raged like a fire, converting where it had not consumed. But having despised, corrupted or enfeebled the Churches at home, Hitler had no exportable religion to ameliorate the rigors of conquest and to suggest to the ordinary man that even if this world is harsh, there are better things in the next. As for the rule of law, he sedulously destroyed it even within the Reich: what prospects were there of even-handed justice for the serfs of the Teutonic dominions?

These are not the indices which guarantee stability for an empire on which the sun will take a long time to set. They are signs, rather, of ultimate disintegration—indeed, of revolution. Clearly Hitler could establish and maintain, for a time, a helot society. But human beings have greater needs, and humanity, in the end, will assert itself. The sword cannot subdue the spirit forever, and for Hitler to have assumed that his Aryan overlords* could have sustained hegemony on the scale

* See *Table Talk*, July 27, 1941, for his extended reflections about the "soldier-peasants" who would form his colonists. One sees mutiny latent in the ruling that they were not to marry townswomen.

he envisaged long enough for it to develop into anything worth the name of empire was a radical failure of historical imagination.* He was doomed before the first of his *Panzer* divisions moved. A by-product himself of the revolution of 1918, he studied too superficially the reasons that make men rebel. Though he was prone to remarks like "a man who has no sense of history is like a man who has no ears or eyes," and though he declared that "I often wonder why the Ancient World collapsed," his sense of the past was banal, vapid and irremediably inaccurate.

If Hitler lacked the historical awareness that might have enabled him to raise his sights and scan the future, he was equally blind to more immediate needs. For who, one might reasonably ask, was going to run the show? The passage in *Mein Kampf* which mentions "the programmatic thinker" continues: "The protest of the present generation, which does not understand him, wrestles with the recognition of posterity, for which he also works." The prose is opaque; but at least it raises the question, how will the empire be governed when posterity has succeeded Hitler, his generals and the party barons? The limits he set himself were always those of his own lifetime. That frenetic activity which starts in 1933 and races forward with increasing momentum derives its energy from a single, obsessive preoccupation: all Hitler's objectives must be attained before he dies.

Time was at once his activator and his enemy. He dreaded its passage. Early in the war he would talk about having only ten years to live. In the records of his sayings kept by Bormann there is an outburst in February, 1945, during which (after regretting that he had started the war a year too late) Hitler laments: "I must now disastrously accomplish everything within the short span of a human life . . . where others had an eternity at their disposal, I only have a few miserable years. The others know that they will have successors." Yet this was the man who, in his public speeches and private pep talks to his generals, repeated over and over again that he, and only he, was capable of fulfilling Germany's destiny; that he alone had the strength of will to complete "that Cyclopean task which the building of an Empire means for a single man."

It is the sound of a man whistling to calm his nerves. Long before

* Yet his views were explicit. "As for the ridiculous hundred million Slavs, we will mould the best of them to the shape that suits us, and we will isolate the rest of them in their own pigsties; and anyone who talks about cherishing the local inhabitant and civilizing him goes straight off into a concentration camp!" *Table Talk,* August 6, 1942.

the wartime degeneration of his health at the hands of that former specialist in venereal disease, Professor Morell (who from 1936 onward acted as his personal physician and, according to Trevor-Roper's *The Last Days of Hitler,* stuffed him with no less than 28 different drugs including compounds of strychnine and belladonna, aphrodisiacs and dangerous sulphonamides), [3] Hitler knew that his life was perpetually at risk. An instinct quickened by his own devious experience as a conspirator warned him that at any time an assassin's bullet or some secret coup might summarily conclude that heroic career. And for these intimations of mortality he had more reasons than he realized, though the precautions he took were always elaborate—so much so that, in the end, Gestapo preparations in advance of a public appearance made it virtually impossible for a killer to get close to him. And this, no doubt, was one of the factors which prevented him from appearing spontaneously, like Churchill, in some bomb-shattered city or even in the forward areas of the battlefield. He trusted neither his fellow citizens nor his army.

But as early as 1933 two attacks were planned: a Königsberg Communist called Lutter, who intended to use a bomb at a political meeting, was apprehended but ultimately released for lack of evidence. In 1935 a Yugoslav Jew in Switzerland, David Frankfurter, had a similar plan. In March, 1937, Helmut Hirsch, another Jew from Stuttgart, was beheaded for preparing a bomb assault in the Nuremberg Stadium. In 1938 three Danzigers were also beheaded for "preparation of treason against the government and crimes involving explosives." That same year a Swiss theological student, Maurice Bavaud, tried to kill Hitler in Munich: a people's court condemned him to death in December and he was executed in May, 1941. Then there was Beppo Römer, one-time captain in the Free Corps, who from 1939 to 1942 watched Hitler's movements with assassination in mind, only to be arrested in February, 1942, on general charges of conspiracy and executed, with forty others, later in the year. And behind such individual initiatives there was a more sinister threat: the well-documented collusion of his generals who, fearful of his military intentions as early as 1938 and 1939, were intermittently scheming to remove him from power, at the least, if not to eliminate him.[4]

Only thirteen minutes saved Hitler's life on November 8, 1939, when a bomb exploded inside a pillar in the restaurant in Munich beside which he had just delivered his annual address commemorating the *Putsch* of 1923. His speech normally ended about 10 P.M., but he left at 9:07 to catch his special train. The bomb exploded at 9:20, killing and injuring a number of the Old Fighters. All the tender persuasion of the Gestapo failed to extract from the ex-Communist Georg Elser, who inserted the bomb, that this was anything other than a private venture.

As the war advanced, however, more complicated strands of opposition ramified, until they came together in the climacteric act of July 20, 1944. The bomb planted in Stauffenberg's briefcase blew to pieces the aspirations of the plotters rather than Hitler and his entourage, but there had been earlier attempts from some of which Hitler escaped by the narrowest of margins. Eugen Gerstenmaier and Fritz-Dietlof Graf von der Schulenburg, for example, intended to shoot Hitler during the victory parade in Paris in July, 1940, but Hitler only made an unannounced and lightning visit. In May, 1941, Paris was again the setting. Hitler was to be shot at his saluting base while taking a parade down the Champs-Elysées, and Graf Schwerin was standing by to hurl a bomb from a balcony. But Hitler never arrived. More than one attempt was made to lure him to Army Group Centre in Russia (the heart of the military side of the conspiracy) so that he could be arrested or shot.

Perhaps his closest shave was on March 7, 1943, when Fabian von Schlabrendorff contrived to plant an explosive device (disguised as a parcel for a colonel in army headquarters, OKH) in an aircraft carrying Hitler from Smolensk to his command post at Rastenburg. The bomb failed to function, yet when by a miracle Schlabrendorff recovered the parcel intact he found that the acid which was supposed to eat through a wire, and thus release the striker on the detonator, had functioned correctly. The striker had been activated, and there were burn marks on the detonator and its cap. Only a fortnight later, on March 21, Colonel von Gersdorff was fully prepared to blow up himself and Hitler (with a British "clam"-type bomb) at a ceremony in a museum which had been the old *Unter den Linden* Armory in Berlin. But again Hitler was preserved by chance or intuition: he ignored his timetable, dashed through the exhibition and gave no opportunity to the self-sacrificial Gersdorff.

And yet, in spite of this constant and evident vulnerability, Hitler never took any steps to ensure the succession. There was no deputy or vice-führer to step smoothly into his shoes as Truman stepped into Roosevelt's. Göring? The thought was increasingly incredible. Nor was the party itself so structured that some form of empowered politburo could handle (at whatever internecine cost) the problem of holding Germany steady, and producing with sufficient speed a new leader, after Hitler's demise. Moreover, it is evident that Hitler never thought seriously or deeply about a sinister possibility to which we will recur—the possibility that he was a Frankenstein who would be consumed by his self-created monster, and that Himmler, having expanded his SS to the dimensions of a state within the state, might one day want to take over the state itself. The simple fact is that the pivot of his marvelous Teutonic empire was his own life. All flesh is grass, even Hitler's, and such slapdash arrangements for the early years of the empire's growth and consolidation meant that on his death, if not before, it was certain to collapse from inner tensions, power struggles, and local fragmentation. In the most important respect, control at the top, the Thousand Year Reich was doomed from the start.

In any case, what kind of empire was on offer?

> Tu regere imperio populos, Romane, memento
> (Hae tibi erunt artes) pacisque imponere morem,
> Parcere subiectis et debellare superbos.*

There was to be nothing like that magnificent injunction from the sixth book of Virgil's *Aeneid*. Instead, its heart was to be of stone . . . literally, for Speer was building and would continue to build in Berlin† those ponderous ziggurats "consciously designed to show off Hitler's power: that vast *Reich Kanzlei* with its huge, echoing marble corridors and ranks of heel-clicking, black-clad sentries, its huge 'study'—in which Hitler felt extremely uncomfortable—and enormous *Adolf-Hitler-Platz* designed either for million-strong, cheering crowds or, Haussman-like, for the day when the regime became unpopular."[5]

Then there was the plan, enduring from before the war, to convert Linz into a town surpassing Vienna—though by pretentiousness rather than elegance. Here Hitler aimed to spend his last years, and of the 125 sketches for the project a quarter were in his own hand. Its delights, Speer records, were to include "a town hall, a large theatre, a military headquarters, a stadium, a picture gallery, a library, a museum of

* Roman, be this thy care—these thine arts—to bear dominion over the nations and to impose the law of peace, to spare the humbled and to war down the proud!

† The decree "Berlin is to be given the style commensurate with the grandeur of our victory" was antedated June 25, 1940, the day of the French armistice. Hitler's particular purpose was to surpass the beauty of Paris!

armaments.'' (The pictures were selected from large leather-bound catalogues delivered to Obersalzberg in 1941—photographs of paintings stolen from Jewish owners by Rosenberg and his Paris office.) Early in the war many other cities were scheduled for similar ''reconstruction'': Nuremberg, Munich, Hanover, Augsburg, Bremen, Weimar and over 20 more. But as the war crumbled it was Giessler, head architect of Linz, who was chiefly summoned to present his designs to the Führer, and it was in one of the party buildings in Linz that a place was reserved for Hitler's tomb, successor or no successor.[6]

Not only are these grandiose schemes a telling example of how Hitler's personal predilections interfered with the efficient conduct of the war*; they are a paradigm of the shape that the empire would take. Interminable miles of bleak *Autobahnen* would stretch like the great American motorways far to the east (''Just think,'' Hitler used to say, ''of being able to drive all the way to the Crimea''), and at appropriate intervals ''Germanic'' cities would be established each with its mock-heroic, statuesque architecture, the surrounding countryside being tilled by presumably happy ''Germanic'' colonies (though the colonial idea failed disastrously in Poland). Somewhere in the picture are the previous inhabitants, or such as have not been eliminated, reduced to a condition of serfdom beside which that of a nineteenth-century Russian would seem paradisal. It was not according to such concepts that the Roman Empire flowered, or the British, or that under Islamic rule Spain became one of the most advanced and civilized centers of Europe.

The pervasive lack of realism and the intention that the ''lords of the universe'' should keep the lower orders in their place are most vividly illustrated from many points of view by the concept of The Train. This notion, which never left the drawing board, was apparently initiated by Todt and comprised a double-decker transcontinental rail system, on a gauge of 9 ft. 10 ins. and with engines and carriages the size of houses but capable of traveling at over 150 mph. The Seine was thus to be linked with the Volga, and Hamburg with Istanbul. It is significant that most elaborate and spacious accommodation was planned for Germanic passengers, whereas the scum of east Europe would have to travel 480 to a carriage (barely more comfortable than the transit to a death camp) with a minute cafeteria to serve their needs. It is characteristic, too, that the stations en route were to have an

* See Chapter 7.

imposing authority: "the architecture," Speer contemptuously stated, "and with it the power of the *Reich* was to overwhelm travellers, literally to slay them." Throughout the war—another index of Hitler's profligacy—100 officials and 80 engineers continued to work away, pursuing a mirage.

It can scarcely be denied, in view of the considerations raised in this chapter, that Hitler's vision of a great Teutonic empire was a fantasy. As we shall find so often in his career, and so often at the critical moments, his intuitive, devious and essentially shallow mind lacked the intellectual strength to grasp the true dimensions of large propositions, and the creative imagination to formulate proper courses of action. An empire is a very large proposition. By making the Thousand Year Reich his prime objective without evolving even the most insignificant means of making it a success, except by the use of force, Hitler committed his greatest mistake. All his other errors were in matters ancillary to this main and fatal project.

3

THE NOBLES OF THE BLOOD

The purity of German blood is the prerequisite for the continued existence of the German people.

—LAW FOR THE PROTECTION OF GERMAN BLOOD AND GERMAN HONOR, *September 15, 1933*

"It *is* a moral issue." The heading to that famous leader in the London *Times* must be one's first and inevitable reaction as one reflects on the course of the Final Solution. There is no possible angle, however oblique, from which it presents a mitigating aspect. The horror is absolute, and as one recalls the dreadful domesticity of the death camps, those piles of gold tooth fillings and the wafer-thin bones of the survivors, one is reduced to the condition of the war poet as he wrote

When you see millions of the mouthless dead
Across your dreams in pale battalions go.

But in an objective assessment of Hitler's performance as a would-be warlord and empire-builder the central question is not whether the Holocaust was immoral, but whether it was the best option—whether, in fact, Hitler might not have gained more by harnessing the energy, the ingenuity, the intellectual vitality of German Jewry to his war machine instead of choosing extermination. The immediate answer, of course, will be that this was impossible; that he could not turn his back on all those vicious denunciations of Jewry which he had delivered in *Mein Kampf* and on public platforms, that once his iron will had determined on a course of action it was irreversible.

All this is true, but it is not all the truth. Recall the distinction he drew in *Mein Kampf* between the political theorist and the politician: "The greatness of the former lies in the abstract soundness of his idea, that of the latter rests on the appropriate attitude to the given realities and on their meaningful use." Here speaks the Hitler of infinitely untrustworthy "flexibility," the man for whom treaties were scraps of paper and who preferred the big lie to the small falsehood. Since Hitler cared nothing for human beings, human beings were pawns in his game and their "meaningful use" could be adapted to suit his convenience. As he was utterly without principles, the alteration or abandonment of apparently fixed and sacred policies caused him no qualms. In spite of the venom spewed out in *Mein Kampf* about Bolshevism, in spite of all those harangues at street corners and later in the great arenas, in spite of the instant abolition of the German Communist Party as soon as he came to power, it was with effortless ease that in 1939 Hitler, via Ribbentrop, made a pact of mutual accommodation with Stalin's Russia. In fact, Hitler predicted such a spin-around in conversation with Rauschning as early as 1934: "We alone can conquer the great continental space, and it will be done by us singly and alone, not through a pact with Moscow . . . That does not mean that I will refuse to walk part of the road together with the Russians, if that will help us. But it will be only to return the more swiftly to our true aims." It is another part of the truth, therefore, to remember that we are concerned with a man who could swivel through 180 degrees with the self-assured poise of a ballet dancer. The eminent political scientist Carl Schmitt, who sold his soul to the Nazis, wrote in *Der Begriff des Politischen* (1932) that "he is sovereign who makes the decisions regulating the emergency situation." That was the Führer's style.

And for Hitler the "given reality" was this: apart from the lunacies of ideology, there was no inherent necessity which required the extinction of the Jews. Ever since the days of the Rothschilds' peer, Gerson von Bleichröder (ennobled in 1872), German Jewry had attained at least a form of symbiosis with the rest of the community. It is true that, even as Bismarck's outstandingly successful financial adviser (in both his public and private affairs), Bleichröder was never *wholly* accepted, certainly by the old nobility; it is true that the record of Wilhelmine Germany is stained by anti-semitic excesses and that the feeling was always there, latent if not overt (but was it not even in Great Britain and the United States?). Persecution, even that of the thirties, the Jews could accept and understand, in the light of their checkered history. But—it is a broad generalization—so many of them had become as much German as Jewish that the idea of total extinction seemed incredible. How else to explain the fact that when the mass exportations to the eastern death camps started, very many Jews firmly believed that this was merely a process of relocation and refused to contemplate more sinister evidence? This dilemma was summarized unforgettably by the leader of the World Jewish Congress, Nahum Goldmann, who died in 1942: "It was unthinkable for me. I was educated in the culture of Beethoven and Mozart. Goethe was my greatest love. I couldn't imagine this same people will create Auschwitz. I admit I am not a poet with the imagination of Dante to foresee the Inferno—I couldn't imagine it. I did not have the character of a poet to see what it means—a million Jews killed."

Hitler, in fact, forgot a significant lesson of the First World War—though he endlessly recalled his own contribution. The Jews then fought as Germans with devoted and self-sacrificing loyalty. To him all that mattered was that in his revision of history the Jews were responsible for the surrender of 1918. But he should have studied *Die Judischen Gefallenen Des Deutschen Heeres, Der Deutsche Marine Und Der Deutschen Schutztruppen 1914–1918*, published in 1932 by the *Reichsbund Judischer Fruntsoldaten*. Here is a volume of over 400 closely printed pages of names, units and dates of death. It is a roll of honor, which certainly deserved more than the occasional latitude which might be granted to a Jew during the thirties because he was a veteran.* Hitler forgot, too, how parlous the state of Germany's war

* Curiously enough, and against all probability, this spirit persisted until 1939. During the invasion of Poland the three platoon commanders of the Third Squadron of the elite First Cavalry Regiment, Egbert von Schmidt-Pauli, Count Friedrich Solms and Johnnie von Herwarth (later German Ambassador to the United Kingdom) were all of Jewish extraction. (Von Herwarth, *Against Two Evils*, p. 170.)

effort might have been without the organizing ability of Jews like Walter Rathenau and Albert Ballin, the managing director of the Hamburg-Amerika Line, or in what a fix the armaments industry, cut off from the saltpeter of Chile, might have found itself without Fritz Haber's work on the process for the mass application of nitrogen fixation.

There is, indeed, nothing in principle to suggest that, had Hitler seen the value of somehow keeping the Jews "within the family" and led them into a "national" war, they would not have rallied as they did in 1914. The results would have been incalculable. Hitler's self-imposed loss in the fields of science and technology—where, as will be seen, the Nazi war system often went awry—was certainly substantial. But there is a more mundane point. As Russia took its toll, and the fighting fronts spread around the continent, Germany's shortage of manpower became increasingly critical. Hitler had sent to their death thousands and thousands of men who would have readily marched thither for the sake of Germany.

In any case, the concept of the lesser man was not impregnable. Wartime pressures on manpower compelled the Germans to incorporate within their armed services a polyglot variety of "volunteers" whose very right to existence would have been called in doubt before 1939. As early as 1943, in fact, they numbered some 800,000—White Russians, Ukrainians, Georgians, Cossacks, Turkestani, Caucasians. And they fought. Units of these "volunteers" were commended for valor in the Crimea and at Stalingrad. Their fellows were found in Normandy and, far from home, No. 795 Georgian Battalion was applauded for its bravery in the defense of Cherbourg. Nor did Himmler and the SS, in spite of their Simon Pure ideology, fail to recruit or impress either local groups or bodies of men who had come in from the cold. It was even possible for these former outcasts to win the Iron Cross. By one of the more delightful ironies, to keep relations with the volunteers sweet the SS was instructed, at one point, to withdraw a journal called *Untermensch*! In this new climate of opinion even a Jew (had he survived) might well have been welcomed into the ranks.

There was perhaps one occasion when Hitler could have pulled it off without loss of face. Before 1934 all the thuggery—the smashing of shops, the beating up of individuals, all the crude and often vicious manifestations of Jew baiting—had been mainly carried out by the bullyboys of the SA. For the average citizen it was the brown shirts and swastika insignia that were primarily identified with this revolting process. It is true that after 1933 the SA, having apparently reached the Promised Land, thirsted more eagerly for blood and was condoned if not encouraged by the government. "In Berlin and other big cities local SA gangs established 'bunkers' in disused warehouses or cellars, to which they carried off anyone to whom they took a dislike, either to maltreat them or hold them to ransom. The normal sanctions of the police were withdrawn, and common crime from robbery to murder brazenly disguised as 'politics.' The only measure taken by the Government was to issue amnesties for 'penal acts committed in the national revolution.' " It is true, also, that after Hitler came to power a series of acts steadily disbarred Jews from the civil service, the law and the media, indeed, from the normal rights of a citizen. Yet, given the will and the perception of need, there was nothing here that was irreversible.

The possible moment was the Night of the Long Knives, June 30, 1934, and its aftermath. One must recall that this massacre was not merely the price that Hitler paid to reassure the army, it was personally convenient; for, as Alan Bullock puts it, the extravagances of the SA had become "a test case involving the whole question of the so-called Second Revolution—the point at which the revolution was to be halted—and the classic problem of all revolutionary leaders when they have come to power, the liquidation of The Party's disreputable past."

Thus, when Hitler elected to cut the heart out of the SA by eliminating not only Röhm but also three Obergruppenführer as well as the Gruppenführer for Berlin and the Gruppenführer for Saxony and Pomerania (along with such incidentals as General Schleicher, Gregor Strasser and an unfortunate music critic called Willi Schmidt, whose murder was a case of mistaken identity), he was able to present himself to the Reichstag and claim, precisely, that as an act of necessity he had eliminated those elements which were dragging Germany's present into disrepute, a small group which, as a result of its scoundrel past, had become "uprooted and had lost altogether any sympathy with any ordered human society." Corrupt, dissolute, homosexual, irremediable revolutionaries, they were like a nodule of cancer in the body politic which must be ruthlessly obliterated. And, said Hitler to the cowed Reichstag, "If anyone reproaches me and asks why I did not resort to the regular courts of justice, then all I can say to him is this: in this hour I was responsible for the fate of the German people, and thereby I became the supreme Justiciar of that people." His triumph was complete. As he boasted to Rauschning shortly afterward, "I stand here stronger than ever before. Forward, *meine Herren* Papen and

Hugenberg! I am ready for the next round." In other words he had destroyed his rivals, drugged the army and taken the industrialists' measure.

If, therefore, he had had the *nous* to perceive that for his long-term imperial aims, and for the war by which he must attain them, the brains and bodies of German Jewry would be an invaluable asset, here surely was the moment when he might have executed one of those characteristic pirouettes. All the possibilities were in his hand. His *Diktat,* at that time, was the only law. He had branded the Brownshirts as traitors, conspirators, criminals, outcasts. How easy to load these sin eaters and scapegoats with yet another burden, and to pin on the SA the guilt for yet one more excess, the crime of Jew baiting! As for himself, amid the great pressures of state business and the years of struggle to set Germany back on the right path, well, some things might regrettably have escaped his attention but nobody who could grasp the magnitude of his task would be slow to excuse him. Now, at least, it might be said that the Jews could once again be considered a part of the German family, as they had always been; not with the full rights accorded to Aryans, perhaps, since this entailed many well-understood racial complications, but still as in some significant sense part of the brotherhood.

In hindsight, of course, such a scenario seems absurd; yet there are mitigating considerations. Since it is evident that Hitler was just as capable of ratting on ideological commitments as he was of spurning a diplomatic agreement, and since his personal power in mid-1934 was already virtually absolute (for by now he had paid the army its Danegeld) there was nothing in the actual situation of the time to prevent him from a volte-face, from representing himself, indeed, as the reasonable and reformed leader, which was at least one of the masks he was now attempting to wear. Within many sections of the old army, within the civil establishment and even in the heart of many a man in the street this novel liberalism would have not been unwelcome. The surprise and drama of the gesture might well have seemed to embody the characteristic Hitlerian flair.

Moreover, it should not be forgotten that, though Hitler chose the other and probably inevitable alternative, though the graph of Jewry's degradation rose steadily toward the climax of the *Krystallnacht* in November, 1938 (after which the Jews not only had to pay a collective fine of one billion marks, and even the cost of damage to their own property, but, by Göring's Decree on Eliminating the Jews from German Economic Life, were excluded from all the retail and service businesses where they mainly predominated) nevertheless expediency and pragmatism still prevailed to a certain extent. During these interim years, because it suited an unstable National-Socialist economy and presented a cosmetic façade for countries which were showing some sense of outrage and even initiating sanctions because of "the Jewish question," many large organizations in Jewish hands were allowed to carry on their businesses.

> In the clothing and retail trades, Jewish firms continued to operate profitably until 1938, and in Berlin and Hamburg, in particular, establishments of known reputation and taste continued to attract their old customers despite their ownership by Jews. In the world of finance no restrictions were placed upon the activities of Jewish firms in the Berlin Bourse, and until 1937 the banking houses of Mendelssohn, Bleichröder, Arnhold, Dreyfuss, Straus, Warburg, Aufhäuser and Behrens were active.[1]

The point is that, though by 1939 a process of osmosis had reduced the German banks from 1350 to 520, the textile trade had assimilated many Jewish concerns within larger agglomerations, and the giants of the iron and steel industries, Mannesmann, Flick and Wolff, had gobbled up their alien competitors, nevertheless the process was gradual—and it was gradual because this suited the Nazis' book. In any case, even after *Krystallnacht* no consistent, clear and long-term *practical* policy had been evolved in regard to the Jews. Since 1934 Heydrich's SS office contained a special cell for devising a terminal solution, yet even by 1939 he was warning Göring that "the main problem" was "to kick the Jew out of Germany." Indeed, it was in January of that year that a Reich Central Office for Jewish Emigration was introduced. It is extraordinary, but it is true, that places like Madagascar should have long been seriously considered as dumps for the Jewish garbage. In other words, during the thirties there was a discernible ambivalence, fluidity and uncertainty within the party's policy. Things had still to go some distance before Himmler could congratulate the Gruppenleiter of Posen on the murder of thousands of Jews by the SS on the grounds that they had "maintained their integrity" and "lived through an unwritten and never-to-be-written glorious page in our history." It was this very ambivalence, perhaps even more marked in 1934, which Hitler might have been able to turn to his advantage had he set his sights on the future and decided, in his Machiavellian way, that for the long-term imperial aim there was more mileage to be gained from using the Jews than from abusing and eradicating them.

The cynical opportunism of that ambivalence may be illustrated in yet another way. Individuals, as well as businesses and industries, could be "protected."

> There was a special category of privileged Jews. These included war veterans, Jews over sixty-five, holders of the Iron Cross First Class, senior civil servants, Jews with foreign connections or an international reputation, and others who still had the means to bribe the police. Their fate depended very much on the personal whims of the local Gauleiter and other officials. Privileged Jews remained subject to blackmail, often crudely expressed in such terms as "going up the chimney" or "making compost."[2]

Thus, though this alleviation was never absolute, it did at least show how the harsh logic of Hitler's anti-Semitic policies could be conveniently warped. The running debate over the status of a quarter-Jew or a half-Jew is another indicator. Occasionally, also, influence in the high places of the old Establishment provided a shield. Johnnie von Herwarth's grandmother came from the banking family of the von Habers, Christian converts from Judaism, which placed him technically beyond the pale. But his father had been one of the elite Uhlans, and this together with the friendship of the liberal diplomat Count von Schulenberg enabled him not only to serve in the German embassy in Moscow but even, after 1939, to obtain a commission in the army—where, of course, he was drawn deep into the circle of Stauffenberg and the Resistance.

Alas, from the start Hitler gave more weight to the other option. Seeking to explain the extraordinary continuance after 1945 of the influence, in many parts of the world, of the spurious *Protocols of the Elders of Zion* on which so much of Nazi anti-Semitism was founded, the Institute of Jewish Affairs decided that the myth's persistence is due to "the propensity for individuals to seek an escape from subconscious fears by transferring blame and guilt on to convenient scapegoats and stereotypes." Immediately after the Enabling Act of March, 1933, removed Hitler from the realm of checks and balances, that transference began, in full measure. During that year alone the Law for the Restoration of the Professional Civil Service and its ancillaries expelled Jews from the bureaucracy, the universities, the professions and the judicial bench. By the Law Against the Overcrowding of

German Schools and Institutions of Higher Learning, Jewish children were denied the right to a formal education. The elder intelligentsia lost their place in the cultural life of the country through the effects of the Press Law and the institution of a Reich Chamber of Culture. The July Law on the Revocation of Naturalization began the process which culminated in the 1935 Nuremberg Laws which limited citizenship to those of Aryan stock and the Law for the Protection of German Blood and German Honor which laid down that "the purity of German blood is the prerequisite for the continued existence of the German people." By 1939 the German Jews were like a patient on the operating table, stripped down to the buff and passively awaiting the knife, but with little hope that when the clinical blow was struck it would be therapeutic.

Nor, of course, was it, for now the long litany of pain began. Even before the decisive Wannsee Conference on January 20, 1942, the first gas murders had taken place (at Chelmno, on December 8, 1941, by carbon monoxide in the back of lorries). Belzec followed and, in May, 1942, Sobibor in east Poland. Auschwitz by now was also in full gear: "Slovak and some French Jews came in March, 1942. The Dutch in July, the Belgian and Yugoslav in August, the Czech in October, the Norwegian and German in December, 1942." According to a report submitted to Himmler by the SS Inspector of Statistics in March, 1943, the number of Jews already extinguished amounted to a minimum of two and a half million, though something like three million is probably a more accurate figure. By the end of the war there were, at best, only about 50,000 Jews left in Germany, and fewer in Austria.

This is not the place—and it would be an interminable record anyway—to chronicle in full the history of the Holocaust. What is relevant is to note that it was not merely a German phenomenon, a fact which bears directly on the argument of this book. Every conquered country, even down to the entrails of Vichy France, helped to swell a total of Jews exterminated in Europe between September, 1939, and May, 1945, which amounted to approximately 6,000,000. (The true figures will never be established: many young children were killed without trace, and it seems that a quantity of smaller communities in the east were simply shoved onto a death train without any form of registration.) But the figures that are known with some precision tell their own tale: Russia 1,000,000; Poland 3,000,000; Hungary 400,000; Czechoslovakia 217,000; Yugoslavia 60,000; Greece 65,000; Austria 65,000; France 83,000; Holland 106,000; Lithuania 135,000 and, among the rest, Germany 160,000. (Finland lost 11, and Denmark, because of its liberal protective policies, only 77.)[3] "The nobles of the blood," as the Führer and his henchmen liked to describe themselves in all their Aryan purity, were evidently distinguished more by bloodthirstiness than by nobility.

What Hitler was doing by this process, in practical terms, was to destroy part of the seed corn of his future empire. The social standards may have been low for most of eastern Jewry and they may have been an introverted, suspicious, independent community. Yet from this stock many creative personalities of the utmost brilliance have emerged, as may be seen from the history of emigration to the United States and the United Kingdom. It is inconceivable that among those millions who died there would not have been many thousands who themselves, or through their children, would have been capable of making a constructive contribution to a Greater German Reich.

At the lowest estimate, the Jews of eastern Europe were capable of carrying out the function performed by the Indians, for example, in east Africa and England, and the Chinese in Malaysia, of the low-level entrepreneur whose energy and acumen bring to a society important amenities. Such had been the way of life for many Jews in Germany itself. But ideology, racist frenzy and a deep-rooted personal antipathy were too strong: Hitler would have none of these things. They never entered his calculations, partly, as has been seen, because, apart from dreaming about building roads and cities and founding colonies, he had only the haziest conception of what an empire would be like when it came into being. He chattered about the British raj, but had never examined in detail how and why it managed to operate a plural society.

It is of no consequence to observe that in eastern Europe there were many precedents for Hitler's behavior. In White Russia and the Ukraine, in Hungary, Rumania and Poland the principle of the pogrom and the practice of Jew baiting were indeed ancient customs. (In Poland 200,000 Jews were killed *after* 1945.) But we are not concerned with justificatory precedent, or even with the morality of the Final Solution; we are concerned with ends and means and are simply asking whether Hitler committed a grave mistake in depriving himself of a mass of people, usually hard-working, often talented, who would have supplied some of the many means necessary to achieve his ultimate end, the solidly established empire. If it were merely a matter of providing precedents, they are available in quantity and sometimes in the most surprising quarters. For who is speaking now?

> The Yid and his bank are now reigning over everything: over Europe, education, civilization, socialism—especially socialism, for he will use it to uproot Christianity and destroy its civilization. And when nothing but anarchy remains, the Yid will be in command of everything. For while he goes about preaching socialism, he will stick together with his own, and after all the riches of Europe will have been wasted, the Yid's bank will still be there. The antichrist will come and stand above the anarchy.

It is, of all people, Dostoevski, writing in his *Notebook* in 1880, Dostoevski whose friend, Councillor of State Pobedonostev, produced this formula for the Jews: "A third will emigrate, a third will be converted, and a third will perish."

Nor do we include the tens of thousands of others who died in and out of the camps—the Jehovah's Witnesses, the gypsies, the homosexuals, the Spanish Republicans, the Greeks and Italians and Serbs and Czechs and French, the uncountable Russian prisoners. We think merely of the Jews, of the many *thousands* of doctors and scientists who were extinguished; of an actor like Harry Baur, or René Blum who ran the Monte Carlo ballet; of poets like Mordechai Gebirtig, Yitzhak Katznelson and Miklos Radnoti; of children's workers like Janusz Korcsak from Warsaw and Alice Salomon from Marseilles, who voluntarily accompanied her flock to the slaughter; of painters like Charlotte Salomon, Rudolf Levy and Hermann Lismann. It is difficult to believe that if Hitler had had the wisdom and the foresight to bring Jewry to his side he would not have benefited—for the short term, in his war effort, and in the longer term (had he succeeded) by the improvement of life's quality within his empire.

The potentiality of the unknown and forgotten dead listed above is emphatically underlined if we consider the actual quality and performance of certain Jews who escaped Hitler's net, either because they were lucky enough to be living abroad before 1933 and did not return, or because by one means or another they extricated themselves and survived. The names come, quite properly, not only from Germany but also from the occupied countries where Nazi racial laws were enforced, and from a member of the Axis, Italy, which played the same game in a more muted fashion. Not all the receiving countries can be mentioned: the United States is chosen as a paradigm because its tradition of hospitality, its surplus wealth, its powerful indigenous population of Jews and the strong moral sense of its academic communities made it fulfill the promise of the Statue of Liberty. Far more Jews of distinction in all fields settled in America than in any other country, and immensely to America's benefit.

The British were alerted at an early stage, when on May 19, 1933, the *Manchester Guardian* devoted a whole page to listing the names of 196 professors and other academics who had been dismissed from their university posts within a period of three weeks. In that same month, due to the energy of Sir William Beveridge (then at the London School of Economics), the Academic Assistance Council was formed "to defend the principle of academic freedom and to help those scholars and scientists of any nationality who, on grounds of race, religion or political opinion, are prevented from continuing their work in their own country." Lord Rutherford took over the presidency, with offices at the Royal Society. But Britain was in a depression. There was little money going spare for the creation of new academic posts. Still, by 1935, 57 scholars or scientists had found permanent positions, and 155 others were in temporary jobs. But in practice Britain was for many merely a staging post on the route to America. There shone the golden future.

For two centuries, at least, music had been one of Germany's greatest glories. Hitler so impoverished the Reich by stimulating emigration that his countrymen were forbidden to hear Mendelssohn and exposed to the continual boom of Wagner's heroics, while America received an extraordinary accession of talent by way of composers, performers and teachers: Béla Bartók, Nadia Boulanger, Adolf Busch, Paul Hindemith, Otto Klemperer, Wanda Landowska, Erich Leinsdorf, Lotte Lenya, Bohuslav Martinu, Darius Milhaud, Artur Schnabel, Arnold Schoenberg, Rudolf Serkin, Igor Stravinsky, George Szell, Arturo Toscanini, Bruno Walter, Kurt Weill. The same was true of the arts and architecture: André Breton, Marc Chagall, René Clair, Salvador Dali, Max Ernst, Fernand Léger, Max Reinhardt and Yves Tanguy, Walter Gropius and Mies van der Rohe. Philosophers included Rudolf Carnap, Ernst Cassirer, Theodor Adorno and Herbert Marcuse. Hannah Arendt was a rich acquisition, and the whole domain of American psychology and psychoanalysis was fertilized and perhaps shaken to its foundations by many continental newcomers for whom Franz Alexander, Bruno Bettelheim, Erich Fromm and Marie Jahoda are but representative names. And there was another. With money supplied by the grande dame of psychoanalysis, Princess Marie Bonaparte, the Freud family was able to escape from Vienna.[4]

The list of uprooted writers and historians is no less staggering. What work of aesthetic or intellectual merit do we now recall as having emerged from Hitler's Reich? Yet across the Atlantic, went, among others, Thomas Mann and his son Golo, Bertolt Brecht, Hermann Broch, Maurice Maeterlinck, Jules Romains, Franz Werfel, Carl Zuckmayer, the diplomat-poet St. John Perse, André Maurois, Sigrid Undset (who escaped from Norway via Russia and Japan), Ernst Toller, Edgar Wind, René Wellek, Claude Lévi-Strauss, Ernst Kantorowicz the medievalist, Felix Gilbert and Erwin Panofsky. A large strand had been wrenched from the fiber of Europe's imaginative life, not to be matched by the subservient scribes who submitted themselves to Goebbels' discipline.

Yet it could be argued that none of these losses damaged Hitler in respect of his short-term aim, military conquest. A few painters and intellectuals—hardly enough to form a company in a second-grade infantry regiment! But this was not true of the scientists. Among his many mistakes one of Hitler's most damaging was his failure to foresee in the thirties that the coming conflict would be a technological war, or to grasp during its course, as Churchill did, the vital role that was being played by applied sciences. As early as June, 1933, the great mathematician John von Neumann wrote to a friend at Princeton: "We have been three days in Göttingen and the rest in Berlin, and had time to see and appreciate the effects of the present German madness. It is simply horrible. In Göttingen, in the first place, it is quite obvious that if these boys continue for only two more years (which is unfortunately very probable) they will ruin German science for a generation—at least." How could it be otherwise under a führer who stated explicitly: "Our national politics will not be revoked or modified, even for scientists. If the dismissal of Jewish scientists means the annihilation of German science, then we shall have to do without science for a few years"?

Yet in the preparation for and prosecution of total war Hitler could not afford the absence of either pure or applied science even for a single year. The classic instance is Germany's inability to construct an atom bomb (described in more detail in Chapter Six). Not only was the teamwork badly organized and feebly supported by the state, the Nazi scientists failed even to arrive at the correct fundamental formula. In part this was because in the preceding decades physics, of all disciplines, had been the most international in character, with constant interchanges of speculations or problems or discoveries between the scientists of different countries, either in conversation or correspondence or conference. In Weimar days Munich, Leipzig, Göttingen and Berlin were as natural and automatic a choice for such exchanges as

Cambridge, Zurich or Leyden. All that was ended by Hitler's own chauvinism, and by the hostile reaction of the international scientific community to his regime. Thus, such scientists as remained in Germany after 1933 were deprived of an important support system for their intellectual life; they risked becoming parochial.

And the quality of their loss, in terms of outstanding and innovative colleagues, can be denoted in a single sentence: five of those who transferred to the United States had already won the Nobel Prize and six were subsequently to do so. It was Einstein who signed the famous letter to Roosevelt of August 2, 1939 (composed by Szilard) which stimulated American activity, though slowly at first, and led ultimately to the Manhattan Project. It was Szilard himself who in Britain and the United States sorted out, by sheer intellectual brilliance, some of the basic theoretical concepts on which an attempt to build a bomb would have to be founded.[5] Then there was another pillar of the project, Enrico Fermi, who had received the Nobel Prize in 1938, "for his demonstrations of the existence of new radioactive elements produced by neutron irradiation, and for his related discovery of nuclear reactions brought about by slow neutrons"; and Bethe, who also became a Nobel Laureate in 1967 for "his contributions to the theory of nuclear reaction," and Teller, who is specially associated with both the atom and the hydrogen bombs. Other Nobel Prizewinners were Felix Bloch (1952), Severo Ochoa and Emilio Segrè (1959), and Eugene Wigner (1968). The scintillating Peter Debye had continued to direct the Max Planck Institute in Berlin until 1939, but he too departed to Cornell University in 1940, already the holder (1936) of a Nobel Prize in chemistry for "his contribution to our knowledge of molecular structures." That dominant pioneer of genetic research, Max Delbrück (whose flavor even laymen may have tasted if they have read James Watson's triumphant account of the discovery of DNA, *The Double Helix*), had also lingered at the Kaiser Wilhelm Institute in Berlin before he evacuated to California in 1937. Other names occur—Pierre Auger, Sergio de Benedetti, and the masterly deviser of the "theory of games," the mathematician John van Neumann, as well as the biochemists Konrad Bloch, Henrik Dam and Fritz Lipmann, all three of whom received Nobel Prizes during or after the war.

We have been recording the names of giants, and Hitler, with certain notable exceptions, left himself with pygmies. Indeed, on an objective view it is remarkable that the Germans advanced as far as they did in the fields of radar, rocket research, nerve gases and the other areas where pure and applied science came together. But the unanswerable question still remains. If Hitler, making a cold and pragmatic assessment of his requirements for the successful development of his war effort, had significantly relaxed his persecution of Jewry, and swallowed his distaste for "intellectuals,"* might not some at least from the galaxy of names already quoted have found it within their conscience to remain "Germans"? To set the German atomic effort on the right lines, for example, only required Hitler's comprehension and backing, plus an intuitive flash from a Szilard, but both were lacking.

It is thus possible (though almost intolerable) to discuss Hitler's treatment of the Jews without any recourse to moral considerations and to assert that, amid the emigrants and those 6,000,000 dead, there were many who might have helped him in the achievement of his ends. But he was obstructed by his obsessions, deeply rooted and loudly proclaimed; though that is no answer, for his chameleon mind could take on any color it chose. For convenience, he could make a Concordat with the Holy See and a pact with Stalin, each of them, ideologically, anathema. Though his nature and past history make the proposition seem improbable, we ought to count his failure to act as a major error of judgment. The consequences speak for themselves. Germany was lucky to escape an atom bomb in whose construction German scientists played a critical part.

* Addressing the foreign press in November, 1938, Hitler spoke about intellectuals. "Unfortunately one needs them. Otherwise one might—I don't know—wipe them out. But, unfortunately, one needs them." This ambivalence was expressed more in terms of wiping out than of cherishing.

THE STRUCTURELESS STATE

Seen from either a stylistic or a logical point of view, it was never a uniform or a logical structure. In it traditional and revolutionary elements commingled uneasily and lent an air of incoherence to the whole. The functions performed in some of its parts seemed to serve no purpose except to offset what went on in others, and there were some sections that seem to have been stuck on in a fit of absentmindedness and then to have been forgotten.

—GORDON A. CRAIG, *Germany 1866–1945*

A country's legal system reflects the ethos of its political institutions. Whether the political base is founded on a written constitution (as in the USA) or on something vague and unformulated (as in Great Britain) is immaterial so long as the ambience is equitable and healthy—and it will be equitable precisely in so far as the laws which are its mirror represent a healthy political structure. Hitler's errors from 1939 onward were so gross that any reference to his "mistakes" tends to divert attention in the direction of the war. But already, in 1933, he had embarked on a process whose results, had he been victorious, would have been fatal. With swift, incisive blows he smashed the political inheritance handed on by the Weimar Republic from an older Germany, and simultaneously distorted and corrupted the legal institutions of the

Reich. Nothing replaced them which could be described as an orderly system of government, and the practice of law was now conducted without principle or that sense of fundamental justice whose absence makes any legal system barren and perverse. The result was a society without a structure and a nation that traveled down lawless roads. Only force remained as a means of subduing and then wooing the conquered territories: the alternative society Hitler offered was otherwise an unattractive shambles.

In the long term—that is, in terms of establishing a Thousand Year Reich—the consequences of what amounted to despotic anarchy were bound to be damaging. It is a characteristic of great empires at the time of their fall that they tend to collapse from within, rotten at the heart. Hitler, however, started to spread the spores of decay immediately he set out on his journey to hegemony, and though the dutiful and efficient Wehrmacht avoided, right to the end, the disease of inner degradation, most of the main organs of government and justice progressively sacrificed their integrity, whether out of fear or of self-interest,* or (occasionally) of ideological conviction.

As will be seen, the by-product was a society fragmented and fissured, lacking common decency or even a shared trust, fearful, selfish, competitive, a jungle world, from Gauleiter down to that neighborhood spy, the V-mann. It seems scarcely worthwhile to dwell longer on the proposition that a Reich so cracked and flawed in its domestic institutions had little hope of providing the firm foundations for a greater Reich. Yet it cannot be too much emphasized that Hitler's mistake in this regard was radical. Millions of young Germans would die for the sake of an empire that was doomed even before they went to war to win it. They came from the background of a police state to set up a slave state. However long it might take, the police state would split because of domestic tensions and rivalries, or the slaves would rebel against the inhuman way of life imposed on them. All this was implicit in the destruction within the Reich itself of civic orders, regular political processes, and the sanitary rule of law.

Hitler's first blow had the effect of a double-barreled shotgun. It secured his primacy both by eliminating the only dangerous opposition party and, at the same time, setting a spurious seal of legitimacy on the confirmation of his personal dictatorship. The issue was the *Gesetz*

* As Hitler fully realized. In a secret speech to editors on November 10, 1938, he explained that "many in the upper ranks of the trained manpower," who had climbed on the Nazi bandwagon, could not be trusted, but that he could not do without them. Balfour, *Propaganda in War 1939–1945*, p. 49.

zur Behebung der Not von Volk und Reich, the Enabling Law for Removing the Distress of People and Reich. To pass the bill was critical; it poured the riches of power into Hitler's hands. Yet it is often forgotten that when the election ended in early March, 1933, Hitler came home with only a minority vote—43.9% of the electorate. Since the other parties were docile, it was the Communists with their 4,848,000 votes who offered the residual threat. When the bill came up before the Reichstag on March 23, therefore, the Kroll Opera House (its temporary seat) was besieged by SS and SA men shouting, "We want the bill—or fire and murder": of the 81 Communist deputies some were arrested,* and others too frightened to put in an appearance, so that 441 votes were cast in favor, and only 94 against. "The street gangs had seized control of the resources of a great modern State, the gutter had come to power." [1]

Alan Bullock's acid comment gains in significance if one analyzes the actual contents of the Enabling Bill. It laid down that the chancellor could draft laws to be enacted by the government, and that these would become effective the day after publication; that for the next four years the government could enact laws without the support of the Reichstag; and that, within certain limits, deviation from the constitution was permissible.† Well might Hitler have chanted, from Arthur Clough's *Decalogue,*

> Thou shalt have one God only; who
> Would be at the expense of two?

Who indeed (if he had any sense) would worship any other than a führer who, in one day, had taken over supreme control of the legislation and the legal future of the state? All the more since, in his address to the Reichstag, Hitler announced that "the Government will only make use of these powers in so far as they are essential for carrying out vitally necessary measures," and then demonstrated his arrogant contempt for his audience and the truth by doing precisely the opposite.

Within a few weeks the provincial government of every state was replaced by Reich governors, all eighteen of them Nazis, with summary powers to make laws and dismiss officials. Since most of the new

* Made possible by a decree of February 28 which suspended the Weimar guarantees of individual liberty, and authorized restrictions on personal liberty and on the right of free expression of opinion . . . including right of assembly and association.

† In this respect Hitler was freed, unlike his predecessors, from a presidential veto (so long as there was a president).

governors were "old Party hands" who looked on their new fiefs as the long-promised land from which they could scoop the reward for their "loyalty," the fragmentation of the Reich had already started; each Gauleiter tended to cultivate his own garden. The ultimate projection of this corruption occurred during the central phase of the war, when Speer, struggling desperately to rationalize and expand the armaments industry, fought a running battle with the Gauleiters to introduce war plants into their territories. As these usually impinged on some private indulgence or would be unwelcome to their supporters they were bitterly opposed, often through party channels to Martin Bormann in Hitler's office, where they were aborted. This decentralization of control is a classic example of how Hitler's policy of fragmentation corrupted the Reich from within and allowed the national good to be subordinated to private interest.

The Hitler state took on a definitive form at an early stage, and another of the long-term consequences of the first false moves may be illustrated by a curious quotation, from a Reichstag decree of April 26, 1942. This states that "the Führer must be in a position to force, with all the means at his disposal, every German, if necessary, whether he be common soldier or officer, low or high official or judge, leading or subordinate official of the party, worker or employer, to fulfill his duties. In case of violation of their duties the Führer is entitled, regardless of rights, to mete out punishment and remove the offender from his post, rank and position without introducing prescribed procedures." This in the middle of a world war! It is impossible to conceive of Churchill or Roosevelt, at such a time, requiring or demanding such powers.

The extraordinary and demeaning authority granted to the great dictator can be explained in a single word, *Märzgefallen,* the word coined to describe those who conveniently joined the Nazi Party after March, 1933, at a time when the old civil service was being purged of Jews or even Republicans; by a series of edicts Jews were also excluded from the Bar, radio, journalism, and musical or theatrical engagements. In business and industry the ax fell also. Old party members or new bandwagon climbers hastened (there were 6,000,000 unemployed) to find themselves a niche—and favoritism, "loyalty" or "usefulness" were always more important considerations than efficiency.* Thus by 1942, and under the stress of war, the chickens

* The careful conformity of such characters was known as *Kadavergehorsam,* the obedience of a corpse.

came home to roost. The "spoils" system, as is usually the case, could not create a solid structure. Alan Bullock writes with such vehemence on this theme that it is worth quoting him again:

> The boasted totalitarian organization of the National Socialist State was in practice riddled with corruption and inefficiency under the patronage of the Nazi bosses, from men like Göring and Himmler, down to the *Gauleiters* and petty local racketeers of every town in Germany. At every level there were conflicts of authority, a fight for power and loot, and the familiar accompaniment of gangster rule, "protection," graft and "rake-off." The Nazis did not change their nature when they came to power.[2]

If much of the management of a war economy had to be upheld on such worm-eaten and cankered pivots, already collapsing under the strain, then all past experience clamors with the question, how could a greater Reich, which would have required a large bureaucracy as well as a force of occupation, have been run without breaking down or a breaking-out? The Ottoman Empire was perhaps not bureaucratically distinguished, but it had other emollients. But Hitler would have had to work fast, to work cruelly, to work on a vast inhuman scale—according to his blueprint. A bureaucracy as inefficient as that in Germany in 1942 might either have undermined the enterprise by its incapacity or, by its ineptitude, merely managed to trigger off a revolt.* The evidence accumulates that the Hitler State was riddled with mistakes.

All this was largely the result of the process called *Gleichschaltung*. "Putting into gear" meant trimming, adapting, revolutionizing every institution, large and often small, so that it conformed with the theories and needs of the party—which in all important respects meant the supreme dictatorial needs of Hitler himself. His theme is to be found in W. S. Gilbert's *Iolanthe:*

> The Law is the true embodiment
> Of everything that's excellent.
> It has no kind of fault or flaw,
> And I, my Lords, embody the Law.

His own view of lawyers, juries and judges and of "due process of law" was rancidly dismissive. Over and over again in his *Table Talk*

* Of the 1663 senior members of the old and not incompetent Prussian Civil Service 28% had been eliminated. In the other states the average was around 5%.

he explodes against them as if attacking some ancient but not quite defeated enemy. "What he needed by way of judges," he said, "were men who were deeply convinced that the law should not safeguard the individual against the State, but that the law should first and foremost see to it that Germany will not perish."

In June, 1938, the *Reichsrechtsführer* Hans Frank put the situation in words on which Hitler could not have improved: "Whether the *Führer* does or does not govern according to a formal written constitution is not a fundamental legal issue. Only the question whether the *Führer,* through his activity, safeguards the life of the Nation is the fundamental legal issue of our time." There was small hope, in the long term, for the durability of an empire whose inhabitants depended for their jurisdiction on the whim of a single and incalculable despot. "I am not even a lawyer—just think what that means! And yet I am your Leader!" So he reassured armaments workers in Berlin in 1940.

They had reason to think what it meant, for little by little Hitler eroded the legal system, declaring himself after the Night of the Long Knives to be "Germany's supreme judge" and compelling magistrates (like civil servants and the military) to swear an oath to his person. By 1942 he had driven the Reichstag to give him the authority to unseat any judge whose sentences seemed too lenient or who failed to conform to party standards. He thus became both the unfettered lawmaker and the unfettered arbiter of those whose duty it was to preserve the law.

This view of Hitler the omnipotent, the source of all authority, had been formulated a little earlier by one of his trumpet-blowers, Ernst R. Huber, whose statement in 1939 gets to the core of the matter:

> The *Führer* unites in himself the whole sovereign power of the *Reich* . . . We must speak, not of state power, but of *Führer* power if we wish to describe political power in the *Völkisches Reich* correctly . . . the *Führer* power is comprehensive and total . . . The *Führer* power is not hemmed in by conditions and controls, by autonomous preserves or shelters and jealously guarded individual rights, but is free and independent, exclusive and without restriction.[3]

And it was true. This was the man who had reduced the practice of law to the nullity described above, had neutralized the trade unions and so constrained political activity that, it has been said, after July, 1933, an independent speech on the floor of the Reichstag, on any subject, "would have caused the very pictures to fall from the walls."

By an odd coincidence Hitler was nearly hoist by his own petard; arraigned, in fact, before one of the ancillary tribunals which he had created to facilitate the judicial process for party purposes. During the Czech crisis of 1938 the group of dissident generals who planned a coup if Hitler decided on invasion intended not to assassinate him or do anything improper, but to seize him and bring him before a people's court. The irony lies in the fact that these courts, instituted in 1934, grew out of the special courts which had been set up after the Reichstag fire to implement (outside the normal courts) the decree "against treason to the German nation and against treasonable activities." Thus the Führer would have been haled before the defenders of "the nation's integrity" whose role he had himself initiated. Munich put a stop to such bizarre thoughts.

But the people's court went on. In every *Land* a replica existed in parallel with the normal higher court, but in these the conduct of business was so streamlined and the directorial powers of the president so summary that cases were dispatched with a minimum of consideration.

If this was a degradation of justice, still more so was what inevitably followed. It became a convenience, and then a habit, for the people's court to get involved with the Gestapo—a source of camp-fodder and so on. Finally the courts developed into one of the Gestapo's full-time agencies. Then, with the coming of Freisler, they slid rapidly down the slope which ended, after the July 20, 1944 plot, in a demonstration of viciously inequitable, humiliating, hysterically merciless condemnations without any of the conditions for a fair hearing, a performance etched into the history of inhumanity.

What sort of men carried justice in their hands in the Third Reich? Let us take, first, the Reich minister of justice for 1932 to 1941—the period during which the law in Germany truly became an ass—Franz Gürtner, 1881–1941. His roots were firm, in that during the 1924 Beer Hall *Putsch* he had greatly assisted Hitler and facilitated his release from the Landsberg prison. Yet, curiously enough, he was one of the few who felt pangs of guilt over what was asked of him. His long record of protest against torture, beating-up and shooting in the concentration camps is an unusual one. But the Gestapo was implacable and, in effect, Gürtner spent his long period as justice minister washing his hands and trying to "prevent the worst," which meant that, during his reign and with his acquiescence, the worst was consummated over the whole range of the German legal system.

His death opened wide doors, for he was succeeded by the president of the people's court in Berlin, Otto Thierack, who in turn was succeeded by Roland Freisler. The attitude that the "supreme judge of the German people," the Führer, expected from his new minister of justice can be expressed simply: he was ordered to pay no attention to any existing law that might interfere with the establishment of a "Nationalist Socialist administration of justice" and Thierack plunged readily into the ongoing process of converting judicial routine into a stick with which to beat "the enemies of the State." Thus he was soon working in association with Goebbels and Himmler (the minister of justice!) on improved arrangements for exterminating the prison population and occupants of the concentration camps. The extreme came when he agreed that Jews, Poles, gypsies, Russians and Ukrainians could be condemned to death by Himmler *without a sentence in the courts*. A nadir had been reached—not surprisingly, in view of Thierack's letter to Bormann of October 13, 1942: "The administration of justice can make only a small contribution to the extermination of these peoples. No useful purpose is served by keeping such persons for years in German prisons." Thierack avoided trial at Nuremberg by hanging himself.

The image of Freisler that persists is of a figure in a blood-red robe, who, by a gesture, sets a hidden camera in action, and then begins to scream a foul-mouthed litany of accusation and humiliation against the proud and, usually, unbroken July 20 plotter standing in front of him, clasping his trousers or otherwise degraded. He had traveled a long way since, in the First World War, he learned Russian, became a commissar and actually a Communist while serving as a prisoner in Siberia. But by 1942 he was a practicing lawyer in Kassel and safely enrolled as a Nazi. This combination led him, step by step, up the ladder of promotion in the Ministry of Justice, and it is worth noting that as a state secretary he represented the ministry at the Wannsee Conference in January, 1942, which gave impetus to the Final Solution. Well before the summer of 1944 he had made his people's court a forum for sadistic abuse and had earned the title "the hanging judge." He was killed by a bomb that fell on the court in February, 1945.

With friends like these, it might well be asked, what need had justice of enemies?

As to that, Hitler was his own worst enemy, creating situations and organizations whose very character was inimical to success. Built into his temperament was the need to duplicate systems so that he could play the manager of one off against the head of the other, or so that one functionary could put in defamatory reports against the other. He was always searching for a kind of political servo-mechanism, which would protect him by its compensatory self-balancing. Both in peace and in war the history of his Reich reveals this phenomenon over and over again, making it difficult to select examples. A possible answer seems to be to choose one case very close to Hitler himself, and then one which shows clearly how distrust and suspicion of his subordinates within a particular organization led him into unnecessary complication. The first case relates to his personal control of the Reich's administration.

The literature about the Hitler period refers frequently to a "State Secretary" as "head of the Reich Chancellery," Lammers. And such indeed was the role of Honorary SS General Hans Heinrich Lammers. But the fact is that there were no less than *three* chancelleries, all set up by Hitler in his casual way without any particular "job prescription." A good lawyer, Lammers was used continuously by Hitler to keep the state machinery ticking over; from January, 1943, he presided over cabinet meetings during Hitler's absence and the Führer's orders had actually to be checked by the strange trio of Lammers, Bormann and Keitel (the eyes, presumably, of the state establishment, the party and the armed forces).

But then Otto Meissner crops up with *his* chancellery. He had served since 1920 in the Reich chancellery office, but what bound him to the Führer was the fact that, as an adviser deep in Hindenburg's confidences, he had powerfully influenced the old man in backing Hitler for the chancellorship. So Hitler kept him on as the state secretary of the presidential chancellery. Speer dismisses his work as "protocol," but he was busy enough to be tried three times (and acquitted) by de-Nazification courts and once, at Nuremberg, by a military tribunal. Meissner had fingers in many pies.

By far the most rapacious, ruthless, powerful and dreaded of the trio, however, was the toadlike Martin Bormann who, after service in a Freikorps, worked his way up to the post, from 1933 to 1941, of right-hand man to Hitler's right-hand man, Rudolf Hess. The sudden flight of Hess to Britain raised Bormann to the head of the party chancellery, from which commanding vantage point he rapidly acquired control of the bureaucracy, the huge funds that flowed Hitler's way, anti-Semitic decrees, the right of access to the Führer's person, security arrangements, and an intimacy that made him a witness to the marriage to Eva Braun. The danger of such a man in such a post was that he was an ideological fanatic and utterly self-interested. Convenient though such a henchman may have been to Hitler in terms of his private interests, it is evident that to have constituted three different chancellery offices run by three so different men was to create a realm of confusion, in which "my most loyal Party comrade," as Hitler called Bormann, intrigued with every form of machination against his rivals and, in any case, was virtually the sole channel to Hitler. Thus, at the very top of the administration, the Führer hacked his own control system into fragments. "Regarded at first as a mere nuisance," writes Gordon Craig, "Bormann developed into a major threat to departmental efficiency." And Hitler supported him.

How different was this lax and malodorous arrangement from that developed by Churchill for the conduct of the war, with Attlee as deputy prime minister deftly handling the business of a taut War Cabinet; General Ismay as Churchill's trusted liaison with the Chiefs of Staff; departmental ministers masters, in the main, of their own affairs; and the whole jigsaw knitting into a single pattern! Nor was Churchill, like Hitler, liable to stand back in a fit of apathy and let government take its course. A Bormann in London is inconceivable. It is a strange anomaly that the despised and "amateur" British should have so surpassed the Germans in this regard. Churchill's administration has been called the finest organization for the conduct of modern war ever devised; Hitler's was less impressive.

After the Ministry of People's Enlightenment and Propaganda was instituted on March 12, 1933, with Goebbels at its head (Hitler having told the cabinet that a great combat against "lethargy" was needed) it might have been supposed that, in this of all domains, a necessary harmony and integration of effort might have prevailed. But far from it. It was only after much internecine warfare that Goebbels survived in his headquarters, the Schinkel Palace on the Wilhelmsplatz, until a bomb destroyed his glory.

Naturally any large department of state tends to be divided into segments, each with a different function. But the minister is usually supreme—answerable, indeed, to Parliament for every aspect of his department in the British system. But for all his fine palazzo and his bright intellect and his long relationship with Hitler, Goebbels never enjoyed supreme authority until, perhaps, the last desperate days of the war. Once again, the Führer dissipated power by a combination of doubled control and the employment of old party hacks.

Of these none had a longer record than Max Amann, Hitler's sergeant-major, who had been with the party from the first and whose publishing house, Eher Verlag, had profited like Hitler from the sales of *Mein Kampf*. Soon after Hitler came to power he was persuaded by Amann to make him president of the Association of Newspaper Publishers. Goebbels despised him, but that did not prevent him taking over, in 1934, famous journals like the *Berliner Illustrierter Zeitung*, the *Berliner Morgenpost*, the *Berliner Tageblatt* and the *Vossiche Zeitung*. But it is said that after a dispute over the Polish press Amann spent two hours telling Goebbels "how little use anybody had for him and his 'miserable' Ministry." Thus, by pushing an old comrade with a knack for press cartelization, Hitler created an establishment in which two of the main members were barely on speaking terms. And, contrary to the general view, Goebbels' control of the press, and particularly of statements issued to the press, was so weak for so long that it was only about 1942 that he laid firm hands on them.

For there was another press baron who usurped a number of Goebbels' perquisites, and he, like Amann, was tied to Hitler by bonds of gratitude and loyalty, having traveled with him during that odyssey of rabble-rousing trips which he made by car and plane across Germany in 1932, a venture in which Hitler always took an excited pride. This was Otto Dietrich who, remarkably, held down the post of national press chief to the party from 1933 to 1945. He undercut Goebbels also, whom he loathed, by carrying out much of Hitler's publicity work. In fact he sought to convert his press division into an independent ministry. His personal independence he displayed when occasional meetings were planned at which Goebbels, Amann and Dietrich could coordinate their efforts. Dietrich simply cut the first meeting. Of neither of the others, however, was Hitler liable to say in his *Table Talk:* "Dr. Dietrich may be physically small, but he is exceptionally gifted at his job . . . I am proud of the fact that with his handful of men I can at once throw the rudder of the press through 180 degrees—as happened on 22 June, 1941 (Barbarossa). There is no other country which can copy us in that." Had Goebbels been present to hear an encomium about what was an essential function of the Ministry of Propaganda, his ministry, he must surely have felt that Hitler's habit of organized disorder had gone far enough. The consequence was that press and propaganda, vital to the Nazis in peacetime as a preaching platform for their philosophy and in war for other obvious reasons, tended not to speak with a single voice or emanate from a single source. There could not be a simpler or, in a sense, a more surprising instance of the "fracture and fissure" principle.

The fact is that, in spite of his assiduity on behalf of The Cause, Goebbels was by no means invulnerable. In his *Oxford History of Germany, 1866–1945* Gordon Craig relevantly restates the dominant theme of this chapter:

> This duplication of function cannot be ascribed solely to Hitler's administrative carelessness and the ambition of his party comrades, for there was an element of design at work as well. During the Kampfzeit Hitler had learned the old lesson of divide and rule and had become adroit in devising checks and balances that protected his own position by making the contenders dependent upon his arbitrament of their disputes. Offsetting every grant of authority with a counter-grant to someone else became the hallmark of his administrative practice after he assumed office. *Not even old comrades like Goebbels were immune to its application.*[4]

This was true even when, as in the next case in question, Goebbels was acting well within the scope of his ministerial office.

Since everything else was to be unified in a comprehensive ideological Gleichschaltung, as minister of propaganda and popular education Goebbels logically established, in September, 1933, a Reichskulturskammer to act as a supervisory body controlling, by its various sections, not only treacherous areas like the press, films, radio and theater, but also books, paintings and sculpture.

Now for the balancing act. Though Goebbels' Chamber of Culture seems to have been perfectly well adapted for its unpleasantly purgative role, Hitler rapidly set up within the party a rival organization, the Office for the Supervision of Ideological Training and Education, under no less a person than Alfred Rosenberg, that old campaigner against modern culture. (His Fighting League against "degenerate art" had been founded as far back as 1929.) Rosenberg was of course a strong competitor, for if *Mein Kampf* was the credo of the movement, Rosenberg's *The Myth of the Twentieth Century* followed it closely with its enormous sales and its opaque theorizing about Nordic superiority.

Unlike the press triptych, this combination of two wholly disparate characters (at least Goebbels had a *mind*) seems, on the face of it, to have worked; though whether Hitler intended it to is another matter. Rosenberg's toughs coped with the infamous burning of the books and the cleansing of the Augean stables of modern art. Goebbels saw to the making of very good films. Both, unusually, launched a joint and prolonged attack on the revered Prussian Academy of Arts. But perhaps the cooperation was no more than superficial. Certainly Hitler had once again married two basically incompatible temperaments, for it was Goebbels who called Rosenberg's book "philosophical belching" and christened his opposite number "Almost Rosenberg" on the grounds that he almost contrived to become a scholar, and a journalist, and a politician. What is ironic, in view of Rosenberg's stance, is that from the autumn of 1940 onward a Rosenberg task force was happily at work in France and the occupied territories expropriating the finest art treasures (of which *some* were surely "degenerate") and all "ownerless" Jewish possessions in France and the Low Countries. Was Hitler once again finding a job for an "old comrade" who could simultaneously ride herd on the too brilliant Goebbels?

Over one issue there was no division, and to have set officials in competition would have been otiose. This was the place of women in society, and since injustice is one of the part-themes of this chapter their treatment deserves a mention, for no properly constituted court of law would have ratified a process which amounted to clearing women out of the public service—a feature of Nazi ideology, which turned with abhorrence from the emancipation that followed 1918 and looked back with approval on the restrictive reign of Good Kaiser Wilhelm. And, as so often under Hitler, injustice that was deplorable in itself led ultimately to operational inefficiency.

Ever since its earliest days the party had debarred women from executive posts, but it could do little more to adjust matters according to its creed without political dominance. Hitler's victory made all possible, and in swift succession many senior civil servants, doctors and other public employees were dismissed, as though a woman were a Jew! In 1936 the ranks of the legal profession were closed, and even schoolteachers lost their jobs. Here was a prejudiced and sexist purge without a shred of legitimacy.

Women in industry and farming were allowed to continue, but for them and the displaced there was, anyway, something else to do. Propaganda and incentives—and for many, it may be, a sense of well-being in the new Reich—steadily pushed up the birthrate, a phenomenon unparalleled elsewhere. Thus when the war came Germany had an enormous reserve of underemployed women (5,000,000 in 1941, of whom nearly one third were domestic workers). But party principles were inflexible, even with men dying at the front. A woman's place was with her child and in her home. Rarities, like the filmmaker Leni Riefenstahl or Hanna Reitsch the airwoman, proved nothing except that Riefenstahl, for example, had won favor with her specious propaganda films.[5]

Since Hitler, with his naïve and narrow understanding of women, supported the party line all the way, it is not surprising that even when his favorite, Speer, set about achieving the impossible in 1943, i.e., to rationalize and fully mobilize Germany's war potential, both Bormann, the party watchdog, and Hitler himself rejected a call-up of women. Speer believed that he could thus have produced 3,000,000 extra servicemen, and in 1943 the generals in Russia would have been overjoyed. But there it was: injustice in the treatment of women ended up as military inefficiency. Once again we have an interesting contrast with Great Britain, than which no country has ever been more fully mobilized and where women, in factories and in the forces, were totally committed. By contrast with Hitler's homely ideas, one recalls that Churchill's daughter Mary served in an anti-aircraft battery.

In all his injustices, his illegalities, his sabotage of political opponents and his duplication of managers in the offices and departments of state, whether great or small, Hitler displayed a meticulous and weasel cunning to ensure that these schemes should never throw up a rival to himself. It may be said that Göring was as loaded with power as with medals. True, the Luftwaffe and the Four Year Plan provided him with a basis for action, but he went soft and the swift intellectual ability which he displayed at Nuremberg was sadly lacking for so long that Hitler need have no fears on that front. But there was one case which might have proved lethal.

In retrospect the SS appears to have had a massive monopoly. In fact, when Hitler achieved power it was little more than a pygmy bodyguard compared with the rampant SA. It was the purge of the SA during the Night of the Long Knives on June 30, 1934, which enabled Hitler to devise another of his balancing acts and give the SS its head. Himmler, as Reichsführer SS, was already in command, and it is from this point that we observe the SS constantly expanding, till the concentration camps are its dreadful bailiwick, its stud farms are set up to breed eligible reinforcements from eligible fathers, the Waffen or armed SS produces so many divisions that it is almost an army within an army and, what with one complication and another, the SS itself becomes virtually a state within a state. Here lay the incipient danger for Hitler.

Himmler was in charge of the political police in every German state. He ran his own intelligence service (ultimately to devour the Abwehr). He used the human masses in the concentration camps to establish an SS industrial complex. "At the beginning of June 1944," Speer writes in *Inside the Third Reich,* "Hitler asked me to assist the SS in its efforts to build up an economic empire extending from raw materials to manufacturing." As the war ran on, the Waffen SS filled up with notorious names—6th SS Panzer Army, 1st and 2nd Panzer Corps, and a range of individual divisions including the infamous 12th and the Waffen SS in the Ardennes who committed the atrocity at Malmédy. Using a more pacific technique, Himmler cunningly scattered the sweetener of a high honorary rank in the SS among people of influence. A small bribe, but the German likes his uniform.

What this amounts to is that if the war had ended successfully, as was of course intended, Himmler would have been in a strong position to attempt a coup. Standing orders for the Waffen SS were that immediately the war ended they were to shed their military uniforms and become the occupation force for the Russian empire. Nor does Himmler's address to his men on their future duties leave any doubt that the SS intended to grasp the greater Reich in a grip of steel.

> What happens to Russians, what happens to the Czechs is a matter of indifference to me . . . Whether the other peoples live in comfort or perish of hunger interests me only as we need them as slaves for our *Kultur*. Whether or not 10,000 Russian women collapse from exhaustion while digging a tank ditch interests me only in so far as the tank ditch is completed for Germany.

The conundrum, of course, is whether Himmler's nerve would have stood the test: ambition and power were both there. It is actually impossible to predict what this enigmatic and ambivalent figure might have done—a man who began and ended the war looking like a minor civil servant, yet who in spite of much opposition had remorselessly and ruthlessly extended the frontiers of his dominion. Certainly it is the case that if Himmler had succeeded the chance of a Thousand Year Reich persisting in the kind hands of the SS seems remote indeed.

Yet there would have been a propriety if the man who created the bloodbath for the SA in 1934 had fallen at the hands of the SS.

> The priest who slew the slayer
> And shall himself be slain.

The extraordinary thing, however, is the way that this man of blood and terror could mesmerize and deceive, even from a distance.* Most of the events described in this chapter occurred before 1939—were, indeed, Hitler's stepping-stones to hegemony. With knowledge of what was actually occurring, therefore, it comes as a profound and wounding shock to read what the liberal/radical George Orwell wrote in a review of *Mein Kampf* in 1940:

> I should like to put it on record that I have never been able to dislike Hitler . . . The fact is that there is something deeply appealing about him . . . It is a pathetic, dog-like face, the face of a man suffering under intolerable wrongs . . . He is the martyr, the victim, Prometheus chained to the rock, the self-sacrificing hero who fights single-handed against impossible odds . . . One feels, as with Napoleon, that he is fighting against destiny, that he *can't* win, and yet that he somehow deserves to.

When one thinks of all the Jews, robbed, disenfranchised and maltreated, the emasculated judiciary and civil servants, the boa constrictor's gulp at Czechoslovakia and Austria; the plans for Barbarossa soon to take shape; the redundant professional women and the impoverishment of all the arts by emigration or ostracism of the finest talents, the burned books and the clink of the broken glass after *Krystallnacht*—when one attempts even a cursory summary of these years, one is bound to feel that if, in the unlikely event, Hitler read George Orwell's piece his laughter must have had an ironic and contemptuous quality not heard from his lips, perhaps, since he bamboozled Chamberlain at Munich.

* In spite of the treatment accorded to women, the majority remained faithful to him. He dazzled them.

5

THE WORSHIPERS OF BAAL

The fool hath said in his heart:
There is no God.

—PSALM XIV

The young Joseph Vissarionovich Djugashvili (known as Stalin) spent five years as a scholar in the Theological Seminary of Tiflis. In his childhood Adolf Schicklgruber (known as Hitler) sang as a chorister and served in the Mass at the Benedictine monastery of Lambach. The first of those lapsed Christians resolved the conflict between religion and atheistic Communism by virtually sweeping the Church from the Russian scene. The other, though he had equally fallen from grace, contrived a German compromise, avoiding, for once, another major mistake.

Though Hitler never formally renounced his faith and continued to pay his religious dues, he had a double motive for active hostility toward the Churches. The first was personal, he had come to see "the fallacy of all religions." Speaking privately in 1937, he recalled "the hard inward struggle" whereby he had released himself from the creed of his childhood: now, he said, "I feel as fresh as a foal in a meadow." The second reason, of course, was ideological: to believe and practice the Christian faith was not consonant with Nazi theory—a theory, indeed, which substituted The Leader for Christ. Since Hitler's instinctive reaction in regard to anything with which he disagreed was to abolish it, one might have expected his attitude to have been as brusque as Stalin's. On the contrary, the history of the Churches under Hitler shows that this was one of the rare issues over which he was tempted to make a gross mistake but saw the danger signals and, for a time at least, acted circumspectly. From the point of view of his long-term aims, however, his policy had graver consequences.

Very many abuses of religious people and organizations undoubtedly occurred throughout his regime, but an objective calculation indicates that they cannot be compared with what happened to others whom Hitler decided to "deal with." He developed no full-scale program of euthanasia for Christianity. From the beginning his technique was rather to absorb, or to conciliate until the time was ripe for harsher action. This was not a sign of goodwill. It was the application of the art of the possible.

His first and most dramatic act of conciliation was the agreement or concordat with the Holy See, signed in Rome by von Papen on June 20, 1933. The political benefit was immediate. The Catholic-oriented Centre Party, in which Church dignitaries were dominant, and its fellow people's party in Bavaria were already in a deliquescent state when Article 32 of the concordat banned Catholic clergy from political activity in Germany. Within a month both parties committed suicide and disappeared from the scene.

The concordat not only enhanced Hitler's diplomatic status and improved his personal image, it also fitted neatly into what has been called "the year of the Church." This surprising concept derives from the fact that in the dying Weimar Republic there were many serious-minded, churchgoing people who yearned for a severe leader to put down degenerate art, fetter "free thinking," keep the intellectuals in their place and reform society. Hitler seemed to confirm the promise of such action offered by some aspects of Nazi propaganda, and the concordat, the seal of approval from Rome, had the appearance of a new beginning. This wishful thinking took no account of the reality, which was that the approach of both signatories to the concordat was entirely cynical.* Still, during Hitler's early months of power many exuberant statements were made about him which suggested that John the Baptist had come again, and brought Christ with him.†

Hitler admired the manifest authority and the complex organization of the Catholic Church (just as he later came to admit a respect for Stalin) because he himself was in the business of power and recognized, as an equal, its effective exercise. But for him the concordat simply provided certain political and propaganda advantages—plus the knowledge, which he soon put into play, that as Rome too had signed out of self-interest he could go a fair distance in his handling of Catholics before the Vatican would revoke. For the prime concern of the negotiators in Rome, and particularly of the pope's secretary Cardinal Pacelli (later Pope Pius XII), was to maintain a sphere of influence for the Church in Germany, to protect Catholic youth and, in simple terms, to avoid obliteration. Hitler's Germany was also felt to be a stout bulwark against the anti-Christ, Communism. As a price, it readily surrendered the political involvement of the Church and, as it turned out, its protests were muted when the party's cohorts switched their attention toward members of the faith. Many clergy in the end spent years in concentration camps, and monasteries were impounded, while the Catholic press and youth organizations escaped infiltration or abolition only temporarily. The security services, moreover, always maintained three special departments for surveillance—one over Jews, one over Marxists, and one over "political Catholicism." It would seem, therefore, that Hitler provoked Rome flagrantly over the years. But this time he was not making a mistake. He had taken the Vatican's measure, as was proved even more forcibly during the war years when the Holy See, as is now known for certain, was aware of the process of the Holocaust and yet, even on this issue of massive human significance, uttered no thunderous denunciation *urbi et orbi*.‡

* "Surely the Reich concordat is the only treaty made by the Church of Rome which was drafted amid the sounds of the rites of Good Friday and worked over and concluded while the bells rang for the festival of Easter." Klaus Scholder, *Die Kirchen und das Dritte Reich*, Vol. 2.

† Such deification was not merely a Germanic aberration. "Pétain was raised to a Christ-like position, well above the stature of modern kings. Gifts of local soil, carefully cut into small sods and labelled from their place of origin, were laid in caskets at his feet; his portrait was raised behind the high altar in front of the saints of the reredos, and he entered the towns of the south to be hailed as greater than Joan of Arc." H. R. Keward, "Patriots and Patriotism in Vichy France," in *Transactions of the Royal Historical Society, 1982*.

‡ The Church did speak out over one issue, Hitler's repellent "euthanasia order," which set up a secret and covertly financed group, the "Reich Working Group for Asylums and Hospitals," whose function was to murder the mentally or incurably ill. 70,000 people are reckoned to have died, often in experiments for new methods of chemical killing. The Archbishop of Bavaria, Cardinal Faulhaber, was notably eloquent on this theme.

In retrospect the prolonged silence of the Holy See, during years when its adherents were increasingly harassed, seems monstrous. There were 30,000,000 Catholics in Germany. If they themselves took little corporate action—less than the Protestants—we must understand sympathetically the constraints of life in the Hitler state and remember that, for the more credulous, the concordat provided a framework within which they could live and faintly hope. But Rome was behaving like a Renaissance state operating on the principles of Machiavelli, rather than as the world center of Christendom. It has been observed that the natural role for the Church would have been to become the focus of opposition to Hitler. In practice, its sole gesture was the pope's famous encyclical of March 14, 1937, *Mit Brennender Sorge* ("with burning sorrow") which was read from all pulpits and immediately banned by the Nazis from printing or circulation. Since it accused them of "sowing the tares of suspicion, discord, hatred, calumny, of secret and open fundamental hostility to Christ and his Church," that is not surprising. But the rest is silence. As in the case of his other persecutions, Hitler's maltreatment of Catholics was a moral error. Yet in weighing the quantity and quality of his mistakes, it must be admitted that both in peace and in war he was not practically impeded in the pursuit of his policies by any unmanageable Catholic reaction. In that feline way of his, he judged to a nicety the strains which the Holy See was content to endure.

Rome's representatives were not all so timorous. There is the honorable list of dignitaries who inveighed from their pulpits: Faulhaber, the Cardinal Archbishop of Bavaria; "the lion of Münster," the Cardinal Archbishop Clemens Graf von Galen; Bernhard Lichtenberg, dean of St. Hedwig's Cathedral in Berlin, who died when dispatched to Dachau for open defense of the Jews; the Jesuit Father Mayer, who for his preaching was deemed "an enemy of the State" and ended up in Sachsenhausen; the other Jesuit, Father Delp, who was executed for involvement in the July 20 plot; Father Müller, who for his varied dissident activities was tortured, blinded and killed. Hundreds of other priests paid for their words, their deeds or at least their faith by relegation to a concentration camp. At one, Dachau, the Bavarian nun Sister Josefa used to smuggle in bread and wine about her person for the sacrament in the secret communion services of incarcerated Catholics.

Even while the concordat discussions were progressing, however, a movement was in train which might well have turned out to be one of Hitler's more egregious mistakes, in the sense that it put at risk that popular support on which he relied so vehemently, particularly during the springtime of his autocracy when power already lay in his hands but there was still doubt as to whether he could hold on to it. The movement was that known as "the German-Christians," and its character has been well described by Professor Owen Chadwick:

> It stood for the religious or even the divine vocation of Hitler in Germany; it had a strong desire to stop the Church being a coterie of parsons and to get the working man into church even (or especially) if he marched there in brown uniform and draped his swastika flags over the altar; it expressed the idea that men must live on their feelings, that the deepest guides of life are blood and guts; and was perfectly ready to accept the Aryan paragraph which excluded Jews by race from officiating as German pastors.[1]

In other words, if Nazi ideology was incompatible with Christianity, Christianity must be made compatible with Nazism. The superficial appeal was obvious. In the July, 1933, Church elections, which Hitler thought important enough to dignify with a broadcast, the German-Christians obtained a majority in *Land* after *Land*. For Hitler the elections mattered also because they ratified the position of Ludwig Müller, whom the Führer had appointed in April as his deputy in Evangelical Church affairs, partly with the object of holding the German-Christians on a rein while conciliatory talks went on with the Evangelical Church proper. Then, in a National Synod at Wittenberg in September, Müller was elevated to Reich bishop.

The sinister drift was not unnoticed. Only a week before Müller's appointment a group of pastors, assembled among others by famous ex-U-boat commander Martin Niemöller, formed the Pastors' Emergency League to protest against the political dilution of Protestantism. More strikingly, 2,000 Evangelical pastors immediately signed a protest against the new developments, and by January, 1934, the membership of the Emergency League had expanded to 7,000. At the heart of the opposition was the deep-rooted Protestantism of the most important state of all, Prussia.

Hitler quickly noted the flashing danger signal. There is no doubt that, had he so wished, he could have silenced the recalcitrants as he had quelled the Communists and other opponents—by a visit to a concentration camp. But 7,000 pastors meant 7,000 congregations, and a substantial number of those who had voted Hitler into power were Protestants. It is worth noting how, in spite of his dictatorial state, Hitler was usually at pains to nurse his constituency, the *Volk*. A standard of living, for example, at least as high as the economy justified—a standard maintained against all reason even into the wartime years. (This was practical politics, not compassion; for not even Goebbels could persuade Hitler to visit any of the cities devastated by the Allied bomber offensive.) So Bishop Müller got his guidelines. He set about closing the breach created by the Emergency League, deleting, for example, the "Aryan" paragraph as an element in Church law. On October 17, 1933, the party received specific instructions to maintain impartiality in Church affairs, an indirect way of putting a brake on the German-Christians.

The latter, however, were out of control. At a rally on November 13 they reiterated all the old demands for the Nazification of the Church, which drew a sharp response from the Emergency League in pulpit after pulpit. This forced another withdrawal, for Müller thought it wise to distance himself from the German-Christians who now, abandoned on all sides, lost cohesion and disappeared from sight. Nor was this the last victory. The running fight continued, with efforts to secularize the Church being countered by stern unbending pastors. Finally Hitler decided, in 1937, that the turbulent priests must be disciplined by holding new Church elections. The Evangelicals reacted vigorously, to such an effect that the Führer implicitly accepted defeat by canceling the elections.

It was an extraordinary phenomenon in Nazi Germany for a group of pastors and their faithful congregations to confront the party and its leader without qualification, and to emerge virtually unscathed, without surrendering any significant doctrinal points. It is true, as Martin Broszat puts it in *The Hitler State,* that "in no other sphere of the National Socialist efforts at co-ordination were the Reich President, leading officers of the armed forces, Ministers and prominent government officers, lawyers and judges so forceful in rejecting the alien influences and indoctrination of National Socialism." It was a case of the old Germany meeting its brash successor, and triumphing. But Broszat's point merely amplifies the argument that Hitler's antennae were sufficiently sensitive to warn him that he was being drawn into a conflict whose results, if he forced the issue too rigorously, must be politically unacceptable. But then the war came, and with it other opponents. The ranks closed, and the Churches, as in other countries, urged on their congregations the duty of dedicated patriotism.

Tyrants, including Hitler, make the mistake of forgetting that, however long their rule, they will die one day and leave behind them a list of men and women who have refused to be oppressed, and paid the price. These names stain like indelible ink the despot's record, ineffaceable, unforgettable. On Hitler's crime sheet appear not only Catholics but, inevitably, Protestants. It is impossible to establish a comparability of self-sacrifice, but among the most heroic, noble and saintlike in their number must certainly be included the theologian Dietrich Bonhoeffer.

Bonhoeffer was preternaturally advanced, original and profound in his speculations, so much so that it was said well after the war that Christian thinkers were only beginning to catch up with him. A teacher as well as a theorist, he radiated an irresistible warmth and it is clear from his history that all who came in contact with him felt drawn to him. He was working in New York in the summer of 1939, and could have stayed there, but in a letter to the distinguished American theologian Reinhold Niebuhr he wrote: "Christians in Germany will face the terrible alternative of either willing the defeat of their nation in order that Christian civilization may survive, or willing the victory of their nation and thereby destroying our civilization. I know which of these alternatives I must choose: *but I cannot make that choice in security.*"

Believing that Hitler was anti-Christ and, as he wrote in his own *Ethics,* that "the rusty swords of the old world are powerless to combat the evils of today," he returned to Germany and immersed himself in the active underground resistance, in which his brother and two brothers-in-law were also engaged. He was at Niemöller's side in starting the Pastors' Emergency League, and his special forte was in relationship with men of good will abroad, a particular case being the liberally minded Bishop Bell of Chichester. They picked him up in April, 1943, and after the pleasures of Buchenwald he was hanged at Flossenbürg in April, 1945, together with Admiral Canaris and Major-General Oster, the Chief of Staff of the Abwehr, who had worked positively and dangerously against the regime since the beginning of the war.

Bonhoeffer's brother, and both brothers-in-law, were also executed. His friend and future biographer, Pastor Eberhard Bethge, had an extraordinary experience, for he too was arrested, but his trial was not scheduled until May, 1945; as a result, he was able to watch from the roof of the Lehrterstrasse prison in Berlin the approach of the Russian troops who brought him salvation. Such were the men who were willing to accept "the defeat of their nation in order that Christian civilization may survive."

As was Niemöller. A leader of the Confessional Church which grew out of his Emergency League, the lion-hearted pastor of Berlin-Dahlem inspired during the mid-thirties an energetic Protestant reaction.

At about this time the deputy leader of the Nazi party, Rudolf Hess, was announcing that atheists had infiltrated the Churches and "modified" their teachings; Hermann Göring was jabbering about "finding a way back to the primeval voices of our race"; and the Hitler Youth leader, Baldur von Schirach, was telling American visitors that German youth intended to "overcome" orthodox Christianity. In the Berlin Sportspalast 15,000 Evangelicals listened to Count Reventlow saying that it was unnecessary to revive Wotan because the spirits of the "ancient deities" lived on in the breast of every German true to his "blood and soil."[2]

It was against such insidious and continuous erosion of their creed and their principles that Niemöller and an abundance of his fellow pastors in the Confessional Church fought by word and deed. But Hitler may be said to have judged the matter nicely from the immediate, practical point of view: the Church did not direct its energies against the political organs of the state, it was not counterrevolutionary, but in its sermons and its direct approaches to Hitler himself sought primarily to defend its spiritual integrity.

Still, it acquired its own martyrology. Like the Catholics, Protestant priests went to the concentration camps in droves. Niemöller was tried on a faked charge, released, seized by the Gestapo in 1938 and confined in Sachsenhausen as "Hitler's special prisoner" for the duration of the war. They dared not maltreat him, as they did the irrepressible Confessional pastor Raul Schneider, who refused to compromise his creed and was starved, tortured and murdered by injections in Buchenwald; or Perels, who helped Jews and the families of imprisoned fellow priests and was shot by the Gestapo; or Grüber, who also aided the Jews and had his teeth kicked out in Sachsenhausen; or Gerstenmaier, who believed in direct action, became involved in the July 20 conspiracy and escaped death by a miracle, having been at the plotters' headquarters on the fatal day but somehow contrived to emerge from the charnel house of the people's court with no more than a sentence of imprisonment. In South Germany reaction had, on the whole, a more formal and conventional pattern, but here too it was a continuing pattern of open protest and dogged refusal to de-Christianize Christianity, with two notable leaders, the Bishops of Bavaria and Württemberg, always at the forefront.

As in the case of the Catholics, therefore, it may plausibly be argued that Hitler's mistake was moral rather than practical. The pressures, the punishments, the brutalities inflicted were severe enough, in all conscience, but never so flamboyant, or so sustained in the face of stubborn opposition, as to deflect the Protestant community from its main purpose of defending religious principles to the more dangerous course of questioning and attacking the fundamental institutions and dogmas of the Nazi state. Perhaps, in a sense, Hitler was saved in this respect by the war. Apart from activists like Bonhoeffer and Gerstenmeier, the Church then became more docile, entangled as it was in the infinite pastoral duties of a wartime situation and, certainly after the invasion of Russia, envisaging the state's enemy as its own. This did not prevent Hitler from employing successfully another tactical gambit. Church revenues were steadily and in the end almost totally confiscated by the state.

Nevertheless, in essence the battle was a draw. Hitler avoided the supreme mistake of pushing Germany's large and devout communities beyond the margin of tolerance, though he pushed them hard—and he maintained a *modus vivendi* with Rome. For their part, the Churches survived to enter the postwar period with their doctrines unsullied and their structure battered but unbroken.

And yet, in a larger sense, Hitler's mistake was massive. In terms of his long-term plan for a Thousand Year Reich, the Churches were irrelevant. Had he been victorious and able to consolidate and expand his hegemony, there is little doubt that they would have been eliminated. What mattered was the mass of his main body, the National Socialists of all sorts and conditions, and the beliefs which they held. In this respect Hitler was the prime mover in a spiritual catastrophe. Not wholly responsible for the party dogma, he nevertheless supported, and encouraged by his own example, its violently atheistic and materialist extravagances. If he did not turn the full power of repression on to the Churches, he handled them roughly enough to demonstrate unequivocally his position to the party. He and his followers, in fact, bowed down not before God but before some gross graven image: after their own fashion, they were worshipers of Baal.

Thus they had nothing to offer of a spiritual character to the inhabitants of the empire they proposed to establish. Their own credo was not for export—whether it be the cloudy and irrational fantasies of

Rosenberg or the radical anti-Christianity of the German-Christians. What might be acceptable to a fervent member of the Nazi party had little attraction for a subjugated non-German. Hitler himself, we know, was an atheist. Thus barren of a message of hope and consolation, or of any teleological promise, Hitler's divisions of occupation and swarms of colonists would have to settle and come to terms with a sullen, alien population. The record shows that in previous empires the availability of some form of religion has, at the most practical level, proved to be a pacifying anodyne. By antagonizing, harassing, maltreating and even murdering the best men in the German Churches, and by sponsoring the evolution of an alternative "National Socialist" faith, Hitler denied himself what would have been a prime requirement in the establishment of a Reich that was to have any chance of lasting a thousand years. But it was a fool, the Psalmist declared, who said in his heart, "There is no God."

THE CULTURE OF PROCUREMENT

Vis consili expers mole ruit sua: "force without mind falls by its own weight."

—HORACE, *Odes* III, iv. 65

"The culture of procurement" is a phrase coined by one of the best of the American military analysts, James Fallows, to describe that huge power block constituted by the politico-military-industrial complex of the United States, which President Eisenhower was the first to identify and publicly condemn. The word "culture" has a sociological or anthropological connotation: it refers to the atmosphere or climate of opinion within which things get done, and it carries the further implication that the "culture" in question has specific characteristics. Thus no better formula could be devised for assessing the nature of the whole armament process from the beginning to the end of Hitler's Reich. The atmosphere had specific characteristics: it was not like that of any of the other belligerents. And what is so significant about it is that its failures, and they were many, arise almost entirely from the same kind of errors as Hitler made in his conduct of other affairs, both in peace and in war. Indeed, many of the failures were directly due to the intervention of Hitler himself. In a study of the means Hitler employed to achieve his ends, and since military operations became his main means, it must be reckoned that to have promoted and indeed sponsored an inefficient armaments industry must rate as one of his more egregious mistakes.

In a technological war where scientific discoveries improve the quality of armaments at a hectic pace, "atmosphere" is everything. In Britain scientists operated freely and with increasing respect from the military authorities, so that in the end men like Zuckerman, Blackett and R. V. Jones were working in the most intimate cooperation with the services, whether it be in operational research or such calculations as Zuckerman made for the interdiction of the railway systems in Italy and France. There was an immense amount of cross-fertilization. The development of the cavity magnetron, revolutionary in its effect, grew out of researches conducted in an atmosphere without constraint. In the United States the harnessing of scientists for the war effort began at a very early stage and had many of the same characteristics of free and uninhibited activity—though admittedly, as the design of the atom bomb began to reach a critical phase, direct pressure on the scientists, not surprisingly, became intense. Still, it is a remarkable fact that long before the United States was committed to war, in 1940, the National Defense Research Committee was set up at the highest level and under the executive order of the president to "correlate and support scientific research on mechanisms and devices of warfare. . . . It shall aid War and Navy Departments and may conduct research for the creation and improvement of instrumentalities, methods, and materials of warfare." The NDRC was further authorized to "enter into contracts and agreements with individuals, educational or scientific institutions, and industrial organizations for studies, experimental investigations and reports." It is one indication of the impetus provided by the NDRC that in that year of Dunkirk research was already far advanced on the proximity fuse which, in 1943 and 1944, would be used with murderous effect by the Americans in the Pacific and against the flying bombs by the British (whose own attempt to evolve such a fuse proved less satisfactory than the American).

There was no such atmosphere in Hitler's Germany. Quite apart from the scientists who had been lost through emigration or elimination, the production of armaments, as will be seen, was divided between so many jealous rivals, and the restriction on thought was so great, that freedom in the evolution of ideas and interchange of speculations between confident colleagues, which so substantially enlivened the British and American effort, was at best a shadow.

Before discussing the armament industry in detail, it might be useful to take two exemplary cases which demonstrate how ruinous the atmosphere of Nazi Germany could prove to be even for a scientist of the highest class. Consider Philipp Lenard, 1862–1947; this holder of the Chair of Theoretical Physics at Heidelberg was awarded the Nobel Prize in 1905. But political distractions worked on his mind: Versailles, the Weimar Republic, etc., made him violently racist and he even denounced Einstein. By 1924 he is openly backing Hitler and Ludendorff and supports them intellectually by a publication in which he argues that "the great investigators of nature" were all of Aryan-Germanic origin. Alas, however, though the Nazis used his adherence for propaganda purposes, he hitched his wagon to the wrong stars, particularly Rosenberg, and in that world where influence at the top was all-important he lacked the right connections. So, by the end of the war, he had withdrawn into retirement. Nevertheless, his career provides a model example of the difficulty of achieving under Hitler the "atmosphere" in which original scientific thinking fructifies. For a Nobel Prizewinner to denounce Einstein on racial and political grounds was to commit a professional crime.

There is a parallel to Lenard—Johannes Stark, Nobel Prizewinner for Physics in 1919. Unfortunately, during the next decade he violently rejected the latest thinking, relativity and quantum theory, so that this Ishmael among the scientists found a refuge among the Nazis and a task agreeable to the party but difficult indeed to execute, viz., an attempt to bring Nazism and the natural sciences into a coherent relationship. It is sad to see a fine mind denigrating "Jewish science" in the classic way approved by Hitler, on the ground that Jews are "unencumbered by regard for truth": for Stark well knew of the outstanding contribution of Jewish scientists. But he was evidently a man of poor tactical judgment. Who else would not only have aligned himself with the fading Rosenberg but even alienated the SS? Stark, too, faded away.

The atmosphere that permeates these brief biographies offers small hope to the scientist for the free play of thought, and little confidence that he is likely to gain the support of the men in power. All that the party functionaries, and even the crazy Rosenberg, are interested in is renegades: scientists of distinction who have broken with their profession and are ready to prostitute their past in the service of the party. None, it will be noted, is interested in the great theoretical discoveries which were being made during the thirties at the frontiers of knowledge. On the highest intellectual level much fine work was, in fact, being done by German scientists before 1939, but the pressures of a police state were so great that the culture of procurement was always in danger of turning stale, as finally happened.

Although Roosevelt had no great feeling for science, he trusted his advisers and was ready to put his money on a good horse. Churchill, with a more intuitive mind and a practical knowledge of science-at-war which went back to, and beyond, 1914, responded so readily to informed recommendations that there were times when he rightly backed the scientists against the service chiefs. The atmosphere on both sides of the Atlantic was favorable. It is difficult, by contrast, to quantify the scale of Hitler's mistake in a field where we are dealing with the possible and the not improbable rather than the certain, with potentialities rather than facts. Still, he failed to embody German scientists within the war effort (quite apart from the Jews) on terms which left their minds free and ensured that all along the line—from Bormann, say, to Göring—the masters of Germany's logistics understood the priorities involved; and that was a grave error indeed, particularly when we remember what his remaining scientists *did* achieve in spite of many disadvantages.

Since their absolute failure to devise and construct an atomic bomb was the German scientists' most spectacular fall from grace, a contrast with the Anglo-American success with the Manhattan Project ought to be revealing—and it is. One illusion can be dispelled. As we feared at the time, the Germans strove almost continuously from the beginning of the war to find an answer. And if a bomb had been built, they would have used it. Hitler knew his Treitschke: "One should be ready to sacrifice even one's good name for the Fatherland—but only for the Fatherland and only when the rein of government is so securely in one's hands that one can hope by resorting to means that the masses look upon as infamous and evil actually to advance the interests of the State." This would have been a Revenge Weapon, a Terror Weapon like the V1 and the V2, usable without fear of reprisals (or only if reprisals were unlikely), quite different from the two nerve gases which the Germans evolved but kept in store, afraid that the Allies could repay in kind.

But Hitler was not interested. The significance of the matter was explained to him in 1940, and with more urgency later in the war. But the abstruse nature of the concepts involved smelled too much like "Jewish science" and in any case he was concerned only with quick results: nothing that would not bear fruit before the end of the war was acceptable. He never, therefore, imposed on the whole process of research a coordinating master mind, a progress chaser, an acute recruiter, a strong man who could iron out differences and evaluate possibilities. If one takes but one part of the American effort and thinks of the work of Oppenheimer and General Groves, the contrast is striking. "The greatest hindrance to the pace of German research was the attitudes of the government to science," wrote David Irving in *The Virus House,* and the consequence was fragmentation. Research units owed allegiance to two and later three supervisory bodies (one the army, till the army saw no future in it, and pulled out). Personal rivalry among the directors was heated and vicious. Funds were not easy to come by: the Germans never even acquired that essential tool the cyclotron.

Above all, they settled for the wrong method. "With their boundless resources the Americans had been able to insure themselves against failure by pushing ahead simultaneously with all four possible methods." The Germans put their main effort into the technique involving heavy water, which, besides being wrong, was dangerous, since the chief stocks came from a Norwegian hydro-electric plant which Allied Special Forces put out of action. The quality of later progress is easily summarized. Ten leading scientists were brought to England after Germany was entered, and held *incommunicado*. When the bomb burst over Hiroshima they could not believe it possible, and felt they were being tricked.

There were good men—if too few—in the German teams: Hahn who had done brilliant work in the thirties, the Nobel Prizewinner Heisenberg, the scintillating von Wizsäcker. What was lacking was a central and encouraging control capable of understanding patiently the immense uncertainties in this kind of work, and funds, and Hitler's faith. The Americans did not find the answer immediately. Given the right atmosphere, who can tell whether in their discussions the Germans might have come to see that the graphite method and not heavy water was the answer? It only needed a flash of intuition. But Oppenheimer wrote about the Manhattan Project: "Almost everyone knew the Project was an unparalleled opportunity to bring to bear the basic knowledge and art of science for the benefit of his country. Almost everyone knew that the job, if it were achieved, would be a part of history. This sense of excitement, of devotion and of patriotism in the end prevailed." Few Germans felt like that.

So, there was no atom bomb. But there were bombers. The panoply of the Luftwaffe in September, 1939, seemed that of a well-found, well-balanced, powerful and unmatched force. A front-line strength of 3,374 aircraft, apart from transports and seaplanes, represented a striking achievement by a nation whose factories in 1933 produced, on average, some 31 aircraft per month. Yet, as so often is the case with Hitler's Germany, the reality is more important than the appearance. And the truth is, first, that in 1939 the Luftwaffe was flawed and weakened by imperfections from which it never recovered, and secondly that, in seeking for what went wrong, one again finds, at important points, the finger of the Führer himself.

It may have been unavoidable for Hitler in 1933 to appoint Göring as minister for aviation and head of the new Reichsluftfahrministerium or State Air Ministry. Yet character traits were there at the beginning—and known to Hitler—which would grievously affect both the expansion and the wartime usage of the Luftwaffe; occasional drugs, jealous fear of rivals, a megalomaniac lack of judgment, an apathetic inability to ensure that decisions, once taken, were put into effect. (As for the war, one need but mention Göring's boast that the Luftwaffe could finish off Dunkirk, his handling of the Battle of Britain, and his assurance that Stalingrad could be kept supplied.) The early development of the Luftwaffe was driven forward by Göring in a state of euphoria owing much to Hitler's passionate desire to obtain a large air force quickly, and to the fact that in the early years money and raw materials had scarcely to be taken into account. It was a world in which the great man could give an order with a wave of the hand and assume that it would be carried out.

But there were constant undercurrents of jealousy and friction—first between Göring and his deputy, State Secretary Milch, a former head of *Lufthansa,* competent and hardworking but impelled by an egocentric arrogance and, in the eyes of the airmen, fatally lacking in military experience. Thus there was always likely to be thunder and lightning at the top of the State Air Ministry, a possibility increased by the presence of Jeschonnek, who in 1933 became Milch's adjutant and by 1939 had soared to Chief of Staff. The relationship between Jeschonnek and Milch was persistently acrimonious, nor was it mollified by the former's self-doubting inability either to manage Göring or to win his confidence. It is not surprising, therefore, that after the famous Peenemünde raid in 1943 Jeschonnek shot himself in a locked room, leaving a note: "I can no longer work with the Reichsmarschall. Long live the Führer."

The fourth element in this quartet was the former fighter "ace" Ernst Udet (with 62 victories to his credit). Milch recalled how Hitler "saw in him, quite erroneously, one of Germany's greatest technical experts in the field of aviation." Göring disagreed, and anyway was uneasy about Udet; but, says Milch, "the important thing was to enhance his own position with Hitler." So in 1936 Udet became chief of the Technical Office. With enormous financial responsibilities and obligations to make far-reaching decisions about the future, in an organization which expanded beneath him from four to twenty-six departments, he could neither cope with the outside world nor prevent internecine warfare amid his own staff. So in October, 1941, he, too, committed suicide and Göring's comment, for once, had a measure of truth. "He made a complete chaos out of our entire Luftwaffe program. If he were alive today, I would have no choice but to say to him, 'You are responsible for the destruction of the German air force.' " *You:* together with Hitler who insisted on his appointment, Göring who dared not oppose what he knew to be a wrong choice, and all those who during five vital years knew what was going wrong but did not have the courage, or the patriotism, to speak out.

For Hitler knew all these men. Göring and Udet were, indeed, his personal appointments. The deduction must be the unlikely one that there were no better alternatives—though, politically speaking, there probably was no better alternative than Göring—or that in his lackadaisical way Hitler just put the man in the job and left him to get on with it. In any case, to bring his new air force into being he certainly assembled an ill-matched team. The test came in 1937, when the first generation of aircraft (those which would start the war, the Me109, the Me110, the Ju87, etc.) were coming along in quantity and the time was ripe for planning a second generation. But 1937 was a year of crisis of supply: foreign exchange and raw materials became desperately short (out of 1,800,000 tons of steel produced per month the services only got 300,000). The policy of procurement was now in dispute. Hitler, Göring and a junta of industrialists wished to press on regardless, while conservatives like Schacht the financier and von Blomberg the defense minister pleaded for caution.

Hitler's answer was ingenious and optimistic—a Four Year Plan, with Göring in charge, to produce by 1939 all the oil and half the rubber necessary for mobilization—by *ersatz* methods, and to scrape the Reich for its internal resources like poor-quality iron ore. At the same time, consumer spending was to continue; well into the war this principle was maintained, suggesting that Hitler and the party, for all their bravado, felt a constant need to maintain popular support by gifts of "bread and circuses." The draconic introduction of rationing in Britain after 1939 certainly contrasts strangely with German liberality.

Thus Göring was well placed to move scarce materials and labor toward the indigent Luftwaffe, as he immediately tried to do, only to be told by the experts that the cupboard was bare. Udet's incompetence could not take the strain; one of his assistants spoke of "how much dilettantism, coercion and improvization became a pattern with us." A proper blueprint was lacking. Instead of concentrating on carefully selected types, "the culture of procurement" enabled Heinkel to work on a dozen at a time, and then reject the majority. Dissipated effort and inept judgment became the rule. The story which best illustrates the lack of clear decision-making amid the upper ranks of the Luftwaffe is that of the long-range bomber. Ever since 1927 a heavy night bomber had been contemplated, and by 1936 work was proceeding on prototypes. Then General Wever, the prophet of strategic bombing, was replaced, and those who advocated quantity production of smaller bombers won the day; there were not enough raw materials or enough fuel, or the industrial capacity to sustain a heavy bomber force. So Göring happily dropped it, in April, 1937.

Yet the extraordinary thing is that almost immediately—at first coolly and then more ardently—plans were laid for another heavy bomber! By 1938 this had reached the prototype stage as the He177. Nor could there be a finer example of the muddled thinking and conflicting staff work that lay behind the fearsome façade of the Luftwaffe than the fact that a demand was made for the huge He177 to have a *dive-bombing* capacity. The body had now to be redesigned to sustain the intense stress of the plunge; the engines had to be remodeled; in test after test fifty machines broke up or caught fire. A few were used and lost at Stalingrad. Never were they employed in any quantity, and the Luftwaffe's plan for concentrating on the He177 as a main weapon in the Second World War proved to be a disastrous failure. This tells one much about Hitler's capacity to select as leaders of his chief striking force men of calm foresight; and the record of the He177 compares almost comically with that of the British Lancaster or the American Fortress.

The He177 was one of four aircraft on which it was decided to concentrate for war. The Me190 needs no praise; British fighter pilots knew its worth. But the case of the twin-engined long-range fighter, the Me210, is horrendous. The intention was to enter the war with its predecessor, the Me110, but this was too heavy to maneuver and, as the Battle of Britain revealed, when sent as an escort for bombers its flights could be shot down like partridges. In desperation, therefore, in the summer of 1938, 1,000 Me210s were ordered straight off the drawing board. Its subsequent career was a long anticlimax. Göring said that his tombstone should carry the inscription "He would have lived longer had the Me210 not been built." Accidents, crashes and deaths marked its progress. By 1941 it had been declared unfit for operational service, and it is reckoned that its cost in raw materials and factory commitment was the equivalent of 600 aircraft. (Thus, in the event, the failure of the He177 was fortunate, since there would have been no long-range fighters available to escort it in daytime; it would have been left to the uncertainties of night bombing!)

The history of the fourth candidate, known because of its speed as the "Wonder Bomber" when it first appeared, is a mirror image of examples James Fallows has cited to demonstrate what happens today within the American culture of procurement. A fine, fast economic aircraft is devised. As soon as the military receive it, requirements are made for manifold extra gadgets. In consequence the weight increases, the speed lessens, and extra armament (plus a man to operate it) becomes necessary to ward off enemy fighters. The end product is an aircraft less agile, less swift, and very substantially more expensive than the prototype. But the contracts are out to the manufacturers! This was precisely the checkered career of the Ju88, which began by breaking speed records and then, in 1938, emerged as another victim of the German obsession for dive bombing, an obsession deeply rooted in the minds of the Luftwaffe staff. The modified machine carried a man too many, was 50 mph too slow, overweight and short on range. All these errors were amended in due course, so that the Ju88 developed into the magnificent multi-purpose machine known so well to the RAF and the USAAF. But of the four aircraft on which the Luftwaffe in the mid-thirties staked its future, only one forthwith and one in due course proved successful; the others were, quite simply, disasters.

There was no shared guilt over what was, perhaps, the gravest folly of them all. In the Me262 the Germans, who devoted a great deal of research effort to jet propulsion, evolved a jet-engine fighter which, on its performance, looked unbeatable. A mock-up had actually been displayed on the experimental grounds at Rechlin before the war. Speer heard it on a test-bed in 1941 but in September, 1943—the classic spiral begins—Hitler stopped large-scale production. Three months later, having read a press report that the British were experimenting with jets, he suddenly demanded as many of the 262s as possible in the shortest possible time! He then went out of his mind, stubbornly insisting that this immensely fast little gnat should be used as a bomber. Nobody could shift him—Speer, Göring, the Luftwaffe generals, even old trusties like Model and Sepp Dietrich. For all wanted the 262, with its speed and rate of climb, to be used against the swarms of American Fortresses which now treated the German skies as their own. Finally, in November, 1944, Hitler recanted and a number of squadrons, mainly flown by crack pilots, got airborne. It has to be added (a) that American fighter pilots soon evolved techniques for dealing with the 262, and (b) that much of the delay in bringing it into production was due to doubts on the part of Milch and the Luftwaffe staff that it had any future. But early mass production would undoubtedly have produced a formidable menace.

No form of excuse can relieve Hitler of responsibility for the failure of the Luftwaffe to produce an efficient second generation of aircraft. Of the four chief men he selects two ultimately commit suicide in despair at their own shortcomings: of the four aircraft they select as war-winners two have an ignominious end. The damage flowed from his own choice. Göring could initiate a program, whether wisely or not, and defend it against his competitors in high Nazi circles, but was quite incapable of oversight, of seeing a program through to the end, stage by stage. Junior staff at the Luftwaffe admit they rarely felt the master's presence. Was it that Hitler did not understand the airplane, except in the broad sense of "air power"? Was he overimpressed with the technical capacities of Göring, who had won the Iron Cross and in 1918 commanded the famous Richthofen squadron—with rather more kills to his credit than are now always accepted?* Did it, in other words, seem all right in 1933?

It must be doubted whether these arrangements were unavoidable or whether they were other than a gross aberration on Hitler's part. For nothing like this happened in respect of his armor, the *Panzers* to whose shock effect he ascribed so much importance. When Guderian

* It is significant that there was a falling-off in the quality of *administration* in Richthofen's squadron after Göring succeeded him as commander.

in 1934 organized a display of what was still a primitive and experimental armored division, Hitler's response was "That's what I need! That's what I want to have!" His attitude never changed. Perhaps he felt a great kinship with these brutal land fortresses and their visible exercise of power. Whatever the reason, there is little evidence of those willfully imperious interventions by Hitler, close though the subject was to his heart, nor were the Panzertruppe leaders selected arbitrarily or incompetently. Guderian, the pure *Panzer* leader, was free to fight the battle for armor, and his struggles were far more against the conservative-minded in the Generalität than against a vexatious Führer, whose confidence he seems to have commanded. Thus there was none of that optimistic dissipation of effort which disfigured the Luftwaffe production program. Instead, the *Panzers* were produced in linear style, the Mark I leading logically and efficiently to the Mark IV, a concentration of design which was sadly lacking in plans for British armor during the thirties.

Hitler's intrusions, fatal as usual, came later, when his tanks were deeply embedded in Russia. The new Tiger Tank, specially developed for the eastern front, was intended to weigh 50 tons. By the "Fallows syndrome," Hitler increased the weight to 75 tons. A 30-ton Panther was therefore designed to provide greater mobility: Hitler added a larger gun and more armor, raising the weight to 48 tons. For all his corporal's knowingness about military details, he seems incapable of understanding that a tank column is kept going by spare parts, which he always parsimoniously grudged, or that the tracks on the tanks he sent racing down to the Caucasus would not last forever.

That Hitler lacked interest in the atom bomb is not so surprising when one recalls Speer's comment that "he was filled with a fundamental distrust of all innovations which, as in the case of the jet aircraft or atom bombs, went beyond the technical experience of the First World War generation and presaged an era he could not know." Yet one would have thought that the prospect of the V weapon would have made his vengeful heart glow with expectation. On the contrary, late in 1939 reduction of rocket research to a low priority accordingly cut its labor force and supply of materials. It was not until 1942, after he had heard that a rocket had successfully completed a flight, that Hitler instantly ordered 5,000 to be prepared for action (five months production; or, alternatively, rather less explosive than would have been delivered in a single combined Anglo-American bomber attack).

The culture of procurement of the V weapons takes on, henceforward, the characteristic Nazi pattern. Until the proved success of the rocket it had been quietly nursed forward at Peenemünde under the worthy General Dornberger and his brilliant assistant Wernher von Braun, with Speer looking on paternally. But now the rocket was a growth prospect, Hitler's interest was rekindled. Supplies began to flow. And thus there happened what Dornberger identified as "a phenomenon which by this time was a matter of course in the armaments industry":

> New organizations were springing up like mushrooms after rain alongside the old and tried ones and inflating themselves furiously. In most cases there was overlapping if not actual duplication. All the departmental bosses, out of suspicion, lust for power or sheer obstinacy, then jealously fought for independence. Occasionally a new organization with few but able men in it had the drive to score a certain initial success. This, it alleged, justified its existence and even entitled it to expand. In no time it was just as cumbersome and hidebound as the predecessors or competitors which it claimed had been failures.[1]

What in effect Hitler allowed to happen was for Himmler and the SS to take over the whole rocket project, in all their ignorance, keeping on the original technical pioneers on sufferance. Himmler moved craftily. First a formal visit; then mysterious indictments of the Peenemünde staff, then a proposal to Hitler that the slave labor he controlled would provide a secure work force at Peenemünde. The dagger blow was to appoint SS General Kammler (the *alter ego* to Heydrich in cold-blooded suavity) as general commissioner for the rocket program. After the bombing of Peenemünde, therefore, it was the SS who created a vast underground factory for the V2, manned by prisoners who worked in the most appalling conditions, and it was the SS who ran the great new firing range at Blitzna in Poland.

It is a rational question, therefore, to ask what if anything Hitler had in mind when he handed over the experts who had just perfected a deadly new weapon to a group which, however *sympathique* in party terms, knew little of the higher reaches of science. Once again the atmosphere had been befouled. The British never found an answer to the V2 rocket, as they did for the flying bomb. Thus it is impossible to calculate what damage might have been done if Dornberger and his team had been permitted to continue, with adequate resources, the tests and researches which had carried them so far. At least we may be sure that Hitler made another mistake in allowing General Kammler of the SS to replace them.

But the V1 and the V2 were irresistible weapons of destruction, once their potentiality was confirmed. All Hitler had needed to do was to ensure an efficient production line after the scientists had done their work (and it is noticeable that during the years of development when Dornberger and von Braun were carrying out their experiments, they worked with relative freedom as an army research unit in the kind of atmosphere conducive to scientific speculation).

There was, however, a larger area, more vital yet less visible, in which it may be maintained that Hitler made one of the major mistakes of the war. The area is that of intelligence, the basic commodity whose lack leaves armies blind and hungry. The British brilliantly and the Americans partially achieved what escaped Hitler entirely—the co-ordination and integration of his secret agencies. Germany was awash with independent, embattled, noncooperative intelligence organizations. Because the navy distanced itself from the political in-fighting that raged over the Reich, its B Dienst was by far the most professional and untainted: the B Service's reading of the British Atlantic convoy signals (until they were changed in 1943) was an inestimable contribution to the U-boat war, and its opposite numbers in Britain accord it the fullest respect. But B Dienst was unique.

Its military counterpart, the Abwehr, was as ambivalent as its head, Admiral Canaris, who could never resolve his distaste for Hitler's methods and admiration for his successes. It was known to the British in the Mediterranean, for example, that Abwehr agents in remote posts were likely to be Jews or other suspect persons, cowering under Canaris's wing. Yet when Heydrich, the butcher of Czechoslovakia, was assassinated Canaris joined Hitler and Himmler in delivering a eulogy. He swung constantly between these poles. It is not surprising, therefore, that his service was a miscellany. Some of its members, for example, were skillful Resistance catchers; but the service as a whole was weak in its prime task of reading the enemy and his intentions. The SS always jealously eyed its functions, and Canaris was powerless to prevent a takeover in 1944 by the Reichssicherheitshauptamt, the intelligence arm of the SS, which now placed Himmler's favorite, Schellenberg, as head of the combined SS and Wehrmacht intelligence. Schellenberg had, in any case, been running his own agents for RSHA in rivalry with the Abwehr. It is typical that Canaris ended his life without any notable distinctions as one of those suspected of implication in the July 20 plot.

Apart from these competitive organizations, there was a system so free from Nazi control that both the Gestapo and the SS made continued attempts to absorb it. This was the Forschungsamt, a substantial network concerned with telegraph tapping and the decoding of telephone or radio conversations. When it was formally established in 1933 Hitler's distaste for bureaucratic centralization was so strong that he refused to lodge it in his chancellor's office, powerful though the weapon might be, and handed it over to Göring. Here was another source of rivalry, because Ribbentrop had his own cipher service in the foreign office and bitterly resented what was an effective competitor. But Göring guarded his prerogative jealously. And then there was the ingenious post office team (on which the SS ultimately laid its hands) which, among other coups, unscrambled transatlantic telephone conversations, and thus made available to Hitler some of the "secret" exchanges between Churchill and Roosevelt—the one at the time of the Italian surrender being a particularly important revelation.

One of the salient features of the contemporary American culture of procurement is the form of persuasion used by the firms fighting for the fat contracts which, with the right political backing, can be obtained from the military. Apart from obvious gambits like bribery and lush entertainment, there are more subtle devices like making and apparently justifying excessive claims for performance, or the introduction of new devices which are not essential but have a spurious attraction, and so on. The name of the game is marketing. It is no coincidence that exactly the same thing happened in the intelligence jungle of Hitler's Reich, where conflicting organizations struggled to assert their power. One obvious means was to maintain a steady flow of intriguing intelligence from agents working overseas. Expense mattered less than a good story. In consequence so many gullible agents, eager to maintain their positions, filed so many dubious reports that it became a problem for those in Germany who had to make the hard intelligence assessments to be certain about whom they could trust. For the SS or the Abwehr, however, quantity tended to be more significant than quality.

The inability to cross-check incoming intelligence; the internecine battles between the different agencies; the concealment from one department of what another department knew; the personalizing of the operation so that it reflected glory on a Göring, or a Ribbentrop, or a Himmler; the sheer impossibility of Hitler being presented with a comprehensive and accurate assessment of the state of affairs are yet further examples of how he allowed the structureless system of peacetime to permeate, and render inefficient, his military procedures. Without a structured system, a technique for comparative checking, a careful evaluation of sources and total cooperation between the services, intelligence is a weak and even dangerous weapon. That the Germans had their occasional successes is undeniable, for the system contained able men and the security of the Allies, particularly in the Resistance field, was by no means impeccable. Nevertheless, Hitler failed, and failed almost casually, to produce that close-knit, unified and dedicated intelligence backup which the magnitude of his military effort and his final ambitions demanded.

Had he bonded his intelligence and security services together so that they worked for a common purpose and shared, with a skeptical scrutiny, the information they garnered (in a rivalry no greater than is inevitable in all clandestine organizations: the British MI5, MI6 and SOE were not always the most affable of companions) then it is just possible that they might have identified the supreme irony: those agents in whom they put the greatest trust were either nonexistent or working under enemy control! Every German spy who attempted to enter Great Britain by air or sea during the war was apprehended. Some preferred an honorable execution. A substantial number, however, either from prudence or because they were at heart anti-Nazi, allowed themselves to be "bent": that is to say, under the surveillance of a "case officer" of MI5 they sent back radio reports to Germany which had been carefully concocted by MI5 to contain a seductive mixture of actual fact (which it was of no great importance for the Germans to learn) and a quota of misinformation. These "bent" agents established such credibility with their masters in Germany that, in due course, MI5 built up an entirely fictitious ring of individuals in key positions whom the agents were supposed to have recruited to extend their network. These ghosts were also accepted. Demands for more information, money and even decorations flowed from a grateful Germany.

All the agents were nominally the property of the Abwehr, run either from Hamburg or from the outstation in Lisbon. In its competitive—and in the end mortal—struggle with the SS it is easy to see how attractive the apparently efficient British ring must have been for the Abwehr staff. It sent back reports which could be definitely confirmed. The original hard core of agents had flourished, so that more and more seemingly knowledgeable spies were added to their number—and quantity of agents, rather than quality, was too often accepted as the ideal target. The same phenomenon was evident in the Middle East, where

"A" Force in Cairo also nourished a group of real or invented agents who transmitted to Germany the truths or falsehoods which their controllers required.

All intelligence is a game of chance. Nevertheless, the likelihood of this immense and successful bluff being called would have been multiplied by a sizable factor if the German agencies had been compelled by Hitler to work in a creative combination, sharing and scrutinizing each other's product with the one objective of establishing the truth, instead of building independent empires, expanding for expansion's sake, and jealously withholding from one another the secrets of their filing cabinets.

The advantage the British gained from the Abwehr's detached and unsupported position was at least duplicated by the fact that they also knew what the Abwehr people were saying to one another. It was during the winter of 1941/42 that the cryptanalysts at Bletchley Park broke the ciphers used by the Abwehr for its main traffic, which became available thereafter for the rest of the war. The oversight of such communications was obviously invaluable in a thousand ways, not least because it enabled MI5 to confirm whether or not the Abwehr had swallowed the misinformation transmitted to it by its notional agents. (It also, for example, provided advance warning as to when a new spy was to be inserted into the country, so that he could be met by a reception committee.)

The ability of the Government Code and Cypher School at Bletchley Park to read the enemy's signals was itself a prime example of that cohesive action which was missing in so many areas of Hitler's war effort. Though it was technically subordinate to "C," the head of MI6, in practice it had considerable freedom and immunity, while its staff was selected indifferently from all three services and temporary foreign office civilians, the criterion being aptitude rather than the color of a uniform. And this cohesion meant that there was neither incentive nor desire to conceal or obscure the truth. Cryptanalysts, translators and intelligence officers were combined in a single purpose—to establish the correct meaning of enemy messages. Moreover, once that meaning was identified its gist was transmitted by radio (in a cipher the Germans never broke) to whichever of the field commands it applied, whether Royal Navy, Army or RAF.

Hitler had all the elements in his hand for setting up an equivalent system, had he so wished. It is a paradox that a democracy achieved an effective form of centralization which escaped a dictatorship. Some of the German code-breakers were men of the highest skill, though too many of the cipher staffs and radio operators who transmitted their own messages were so careless that they provided the cryptanalysts at Bletchley Park with golden opportunities for cracking a cipher. Still, if one conceives of all the code-breakers in all the Reich's rival departments compelled to work together by a Führer's directive, with a shared objective and no competition, one realizes how dramatically this aspect of the German war effort might have been improved.

Instead, we have the same picture as in other fields: fissure and fragmentation, hostile barons defending or enlarging their private fiefs, the SS avidly determined to swallow everything within sight, the culture of procurement at its most corrupt and self-defeating. Above all we have Hitler, the *soi-disant* man of Will, lacking either the strength or the concern to impose order where, for the acquisition of empire, order was a vital requirement.

7

THE PREMATURE EXPLOSION

But man, proud man,
Drest in a little brief authority,
Most ignorant of what he's most assured,
His glassy essence, like an angry ape
Plays such fantastic tricks before high heaven
As make the angels weep.

—WILLIAM SHAKESPEARE, *Measure for Measure*

One source of Hitler's many mistakes was his lack of what Napoleon praised, the ability *de fixer les objets longtemps sans être fatigué*. He was never exhausted because he never made the effort. The future was a haze, where he expected remote objectives and imperatives to define themselves only as he drew closer to them. He was incapable of steadily scanning the distant horizon, of working out with careful anticipation the precise circumstances within which he would have to operate when he arrived, and the exact measures which would be necessary to consolidate. The swift and unexpected blow—and then, see what happens!* The supreme example of this myopia is his precipitation of

* It might be claimed that his patient refusal, during the years of the *Kampfzeit*, to allow the SA to go all out for a revolutionary coup, and his insistence on achieving power by ''constitutional'' means, however dubious, provide an unusual and indeed uncharacteristic example of far-sighted forbearance. However true that may be of his political calculations, it is undeniable that in military matters his sight was short.

the Second World War. Without due consideration he initiated the wrong conflict, at the wrong time, and with the wrong forces.

To be sure, he had plainly stated in *Mein Kampf* that he envisaged the vassaldom of Poland, the subjugation of France, and the humiliating conquest of Russia. But "ripeness is all": and whereas in his political forays (even when they involved an element of military risk) he had displayed a sense of timing amounting to extrasensory perception—the recovery of the Ruhr, the Czechoslovakian bluff, the rape of Austria—even in September, 1939, he acted with a precipitancy which was more characteristic of a brainless Hussar than a Great Captain accustomed to weigh the long-term consequences of his operations. The successive *Blitzes* during the next twelve months had the characteristics of Rommel's famous "dash to the wire" during the *Crusader* battle in the winter of 1941: they were dramatic, their initial effect was spuriously triumphant, but their very success contained the seeds of ultimate defeat.

When the SS mounted (with a clumsiness which is still not appreciated) the cloak-and-dagger escapades designed to produce a *casus belli* for the invasion of Poland it is clear that Hitler, though temporarily infuriated through being robbed of some kind of war by the Munich agreement, still contemplated with an undisguised sense of unease the possible consequence of a conflict with Britain and France; even though he calculated (with much justification in the latter case) that in the poker game he was playing he not only held the winning cards but, on balance, would probably be able once again to call his potential opponents' bluff. This was the major mistake which resulted, ultimately, in a world war.

And it was a mistake which was the product, fundamentally, of a failure in intelligence. Hitler should have understood that Chamberlain's spring guarantee to Poland was a commitment different in kind from anything the British had so far undertaken. It was public. It was entirely uncharacteristic. Its very novelty and its lack of cmpromise carried to ears attuned to the nuances of diplomacy an inner meaning which Hitler ought to have grasped: here, at last, was a promise on which even the perfidious British would find it very difficult to rat. The likelihood of London turning a blind eye on aggression in Poland or fading out of the picture at an early stage, as Hitler hoped, was therefore minimal. The British concept of "honor" and "duty" in international affairs is so checkered that on many an occasion a man could reasonably doubt where the road would lead; but in this case "honor" was involved in a way that could not be evaded. Apart, therefore, from the intensive rearmament and manning of the forces initiated in the UK in 1939, there was a scrap of paper which in itself should have told Hitler everything necessary.

But something had occurred at a far deeper level. Discussing the Abdication Crisis in his biography of Baldwin, the historian G. M. Young observes that there was one weekend during which it was possible to watch the British public making up its mind. Between the spring and the autumn of 1939, in a similar way, it was possible for an acute witness to note that, sometimes openly, sometimes subliminally, the attitude of the British public was changing to a point where enough, it felt, was enough. The climate of opinion in September, 1939, was not the climate of opinion of Munich. It is difficult to be certain, but if Chamberlain had attempted to run out on his promise to Poland and let Hitler get away with it once again, his parliamentary position would, at best, have been jeopardized—in spite of the hard-grained members of the Conservative Party, the pacifist wing of the Labour Party, the Peace Pledge idealists and the merely thoughtless. Nothing of this was evident to Hitler because, by his own contrivance, those who reported the truth were not believed and few reported the truth. Ribbentrop's Foreign Service, constructed to suit the Führer, was not prone to objectivity. So Hitler remained "most ignorant of what he's most assured."

He thus entered Poland in blinkers, scarcely conscious of the fact that, by taking on the British Empire, he had no sure guarantee that, instead of the brief and brilliant campaign which was all that he anticipated, he might become involved, as proved to be the case, in a prolonged, ever-expanding and ultimately global conflict. He had launched the wrong war. And he had done so at the wrong time, for in terms of protracted operations none of the three armed services was ready. Whether it be research and development, or operational designing, or accumulation of stocks, or tooling for mass production, the navy and the army and the Luftwaffe were all committed to preparatory procedures which predicated war in 1942 or 1943. From the relatively close viewpoint of November, 1942, Field-Marshal Milch, so intimately connected with the Luftwaffe's checkered career, observed that "if the French campaign had started right after the Polish one, we in the Luftwaffe would probably have been relegated to the sidelines. *The war would have been over for us on the fifth day*." [1]

By chance the biographer of Field-Marshal Milch, David Irving, is notoriously one of the students of the epoch least likely to let slip an opportunity for registering a point in Hitler's favor. It is significant, therefore, that his summary of the state of the Luftwaffe in 1939 describes a force that is ill-prepared, at almost every point, for a long-lasting war.

> Milch knew, perhaps better than anyone else, how unprepared the *Luftwaffe* was. They still lacked trained commanders at every level. They had fuel stores sufficient for war operations for six months at most. The bomb dumps held enough bombs for about three weeks' hostilities against a small enemy and most of these were 10-kilogramme bombs secretly purchased by the *Reichswehr* a decade before; sample quantities of 50- and 250-kilogramme bombs and a very few 500-kilogramme bombs had been manufactured for the Spanish War, but all larger sizes were still on the drawing board. Hitler forbade the manufacture of more, explaining to Milch, "Nobody inquires whether I have any bombs or ammunition, it is the number of aircraft and guns that count." Only 182,000 tons of steel had been allocated to air force equipment in the year ending 1 April, 1939, compared with 380,400 tons for the expansion of the industry and civil aviation. *Hardly can a nation have planned for world war within one year with less foresight than Germany in 1939.*

In fact the awe in which the Luftwaffe was then held is a masterpiece of propaganda. No window was better dressed. Even its Order of Battle—and its achievements—during the campaigns in France and the Low Countries have a delusive quality. Most of the aircraft it met in combat, for example, were even more antiquated or inefficient. Moreover, when one looks at the situation from the point of view of a war that might last for years rather than months, the façade cracks. One realizes that behind it there were desperately few reserves—anything that could fly was "up front"—and a dangerous shortage of construction plants, rare raw materials, ammunition stockpiles, etc.—the logistic base for the future. A force of some 4,000 aircraft destroyed, according to OKW, 4,233 of the enemy for a loss of 1,389. Göring was made by Hitler *Reichsmarschall des Grossdeutschen Reiches*, and Milch, Kesselring and Sperrle became field marshals.* But *sic*

* Some of the successful also received the notorious *Dotationen*: cash awards from Hitler's privy chest or estates in the conquered territories. The well-known financial grants to British commanders after 1918 were in the public domain. These were clandestine, so much so that some recipients later denied them. (A few officers, e.g., Brauschitsch, had received their bribes even before 1939.) The result of these secret subventions was to bind the Generalität more tightly to Hitler.

transit gloria mundi! For this would prove to be the Everest-point in the whole of the Luftwaffe's history.

In the Wehrmacht (until it was adulterated by the Waffen SS) pride of place was naturally given, in Hitler's eyes, to his regular armored divisions. Yet once again, in spite of their undoubted menace and power, appearance belied reality. Their pioneer and inspiring leader, General Guderian, discovered as early as the Polish campaign that practically every doctrine he had preached for the correct employment of armour had been disregarded or had failed to be implemented. He and his supporters found that:

> without infantry to support or even at times to spearhead the attack, without anti-tank guns to ward off enemy armor, without artillery to soften-up strongpoints, without engineers to provide passage across obstacles, and without the supply columns to bring up the all-important fuel, ammunition and spare-parts, neither the tank nor the *Panzer* division could operate effectively.[2]

By May, 1940, some points had been rectified, as was shown at the crossing of the Meuse, but a number of others were still glaringly deficient. In particular, little had been done to provide the tracked transport which for Guderian was a prime requirement.

The tanks were certainly not made of cardboard, as Allied propaganda so often suggested at the time. Still, if we strike a balance in May, 1940, we see how (setting on one side the incompetent use by the French of their own massive stocks) the fighting array of German armor conceals many weaknesses. Some 2,574 tanks of the 3,381 available for the Wehrmacht were employed in the West. But of these 1,478 were the original models, the PzKw I and II, whose obsolescence had already been revealed in the Polish campaign; 334 were Czech tanks acquired during the takeover. Thus there were only 349 PzKw III, and only 278 of the Mark IV model which would later become the workhorse in the African and Russian campaigns.

In other respects, too, the army was ill-prepared. Between September, 1939, and the spring of 1940 its stocks of rifles, machine guns, anti-tank guns, mortars and various types of artillery had only been increased by an average of 10%—scarcely a stockpile on which to base a war of any duration. As regards transport, the situation was paralytic. During the spring of 1940 the whole army was receiving no more than 1,000 trucks per quarter. Whatever Halder's moral fiber, he was at least an educated staff officer, and in February he noted that unless there was some change in the situation "the army cannot pull through in any operation. . . . If we allow . . . for the normal monthly loss (not including combat casualties) . . . production will cover only half that loss." However, there *was* a change in the situation. By the end of April the lack of trucks was so appalling that the chief of the Army general staff considered that the only permanent solution lay in a *demotorization** program! "The most important thing . . . is to start at once procuring (horse-drawn) vehicles, harness, etc." And it is, of course, a well-known fact that during the rest of the war, on both the eastern and western fronts, for the transport of supplies the horse mainly replaced the internal combustion engine.

To achieve victory in the long term over a naval power like Great Britain surely implied a capacity, if not to fight a Jutland, at least to do a good deal of damage.† In 1939, however, the German navy was not even one eighth the size of the British, as is understandable, since Raeder's construction program had as its target a war starting no earlier than 1942. However, for the sake of a flashy success in Norway which virtually eroded any hopes of a successful cross-Channel invasion, Hitler lost (all sunk) three cruisers, ten destroyers, eleven transports, and three mine-sweepers as well as a gunnery-ship, while three cruisers and a battleship were so damaged that they were *hors de combat*. Thus in the critical month of June, 1940, all that was available for operations was one heavy cruiser, four destroyers, nineteen torpedo boats and two light cruisers. The third of the German armed services was therefore in no better shape to undertake a long war. Indeed, bearing in mind the shortage of shipyards, the availability of steel, and the fact that a battleship or large cruiser cannot be run up overnight, one might argue that of all the three services the navy was now in by far the worst position.

It has thus been rightly observed that Germany's strength consisted of her opponents' weakness, and that once again a saying of Sun Tzu (so often apropos after 1,500 years) rings the bell: "To secure ourselves from defeat lies in our hands, but the opportunity of defeating the enemy is provided by the enemy himself."

But to say that is not enough. German military power in 1939,

* "Demotorization" is one of those tricks of disinformation at which the Germans were so adept: cf., "advancing westward" to describe Rommel's final withdrawal from Egypt to Tunisia.

† It was a major error to aim at a "big" fleet instead of building the maximum number of U-boats.

indifferent but still formidable, should surely have been supported by strategic planning of at least a reputable quality: yet the truth is that Hitler's initial plans for the conquest of western Europe were abysmal. For months after the outbreak of war the intention which, it will be remembered, Hitler tried more than once to put into practice (though he was foiled by the winter weather) was for a heavy attack in the north supported by a weaker assault on the left flank. All the weight of the armor was to be concentrated in Bock's Army Group B, which was to slice into Belgium and Holland. The army groups on the left, under von Rundstedt and von Leeb, had primarily a protective and supportive role. The 22 divisions on the southern front contained not a single armored formation.

The revised plan for "Operation Yellow," as it was called, read: "All available forces will be committed with the intention of bringing to battle on north French and Belgian soil as many sections of the French army and its allies as possible. This will create favorable conditions for the future conduct of the war against England and France on land and in the air." But that extremely professional and skeptical commander von Manstein pointed out that "the territorial objective was the Channel coastline. *What would follow this first punch we were not told*."

There is, in fact, no strategic concept here which takes into account detailed preparations for the long haul that would be necessary on the supposition that Churchill might decide to fight to the death: no long-term plan for dealing with a recalcitrant Great Britain other than the seizure along the Channel coast of bases for Luftwaffe bombers that were capable of damaging, but not destroying, the defensive installations and industries of the United Kingdom. And so it would probably have remained, had it not been for an event at Mechelen in Belgium on January 10, 1940. Few episodes in the Second World War more justify the "Cleopatra's nose" theory of history than the case of Major Hellmuth Reinberger of the 7th Airborne Division.

On that day the unfortunate major had to make a forced landing while disobeying orders, to the extent of flying over foreign territory while he had in his possession top secret documents—in this case the plans for the German invasion of western Europe. Hitler was naturally furious, partly because his personal instructions had been ignored and partly because he assumed that his plans had been "blown." In a sense, this was true; but only in a sense. In fact, the consequences of Major Reinberger's indiscretion are full of irony. First, an attempt to burn the papers had failed, and Belgian intelligence had indeed managed to recover the greater part of the documents. To these the Belgians naturally attached great weight. On the other hand, however, the British and French were lukewarm about the whole business, assuming that the papers were a plant. Neither Gamelin's HQ nor the HQ of the British Expeditionary Force in France was prepared to take them seriously, though a few provisional moves were made, just in case. But the real irony consists in the fact that had it not been for the Mechelen affair there is a high degree of probability that Hitler would have continued to adhere to his indifferent existing plan for the invasion of the Low Countries and France. Instead, it is at this point that we can probably discern the first important moves in that change of heart which caused Hitler (against the will of his General Staff) to switch the main weight of his attack, and the bulk of his armor, from the north and to achieve total surprise by forcing his main offensive through the Ardennes and then across the Meuse. His mind had been moving in this direction before Mechelen, but the fact that his original operational plan had been compromised powerfully assisted him in accepting the new ideas emanating from von Manstein. The General Staff loathed Manstein and his plans and tried to get rid of him by giving him a command at home. But he was summoned to Hitler, who was delighted to discover that an acute professional supported on technical grounds his own intuitions. From then on, the Ardennes became the area of the main Schwerpunkt, with results that are famous. But it is ironical to think that without the ineptitude of Major Reinberger things might have been very different, and that the reputation Hitler gained as a warlord depended, at least in part, on a solitary act of insubordination. Nor had even this latest concept a long-term military objective.

So the May offensive was launched along the lines of the Hitler/Manstein plan and, with the urgent brutality of the Blitzkrieg, brought the Wehrmacht to Dunkirk and beyond. "And wherein lies the secret of this victory? In the enormous dynamism of the Führer . . . without his will it would never have come to pass." So the quartermaster general of the Army, Eduard Wagner, who, though he had long been in touch with dissident elements, seems temporarily to have succumbed to the charisma which Hitler could employ like a drug. It did not, however, save Wagner from being suspended from a meat hook after the July plot of 1944! In his intoxication Wagner failed to observe a critical flaw in Hitler's makeup as a warlord: he was too prone to wavering, and too easily ran away from the really big but risky command decisions. Indeed, he had demonstrated some of this lack of fiber during the offensive itself, for at the time of the Meuse crossing, when von Kleist's armored spearheads were already 50 miles beyond the river, Hitler lost his nerve because the infantry could not keep pace as flank guards, and actually ordered the advance to be stopped. Now, as the Wehrmacht spread out along the Channel coast and looked across to the Dover cliffs, the fundamental question was "What next?" And the correct answer was "Who dares, wins." But Hitler was unwilling to dare.

Few informed military analysts, and few who, like the author, were serving at the time with the anti-invasion troops along the south coast, would deny that if Hitler had risked all and launched an instant cross-Channel assault immediately after Dunkirk, the likelihood of its failure, though real, would have been small. For what was there to stop it? Virtually every modern tank had been left behind in France and the few remaining in England were obsolete training models. In the whole of the British Army there was only one infantry division whose training, morale and state of equipment justified describing it as a fighting formation: this was Montgomery's 3rd Division, which that indomitable leader of men had nursed through the worst part of the battles in France and back from Dunkirk, and then, with characteristic energy, had restored within weeks to the condition of a first-class unit. The field artillery regiment which the author joined on its return from Dunkirk ought to have possessed twenty-four 25-pounder field guns: its total equipment at that moment was one commandeered civilian van! The pillboxes and antitank traps which had been hastily started had the appearance of work carried out by some old engineer of the Crimean War.

Thus, if Hitler had lived up to his pretensions as a great warlord, he would have ignored the poverty of his Navy and the protestations of its commanders. Exercising that will of which he was so proud, he would have assembled from every quarter (leaving a balance on the Russian front) the great preponderance of strength then available in the Luftwaffe; and would have insisted, *whatever the risk*, on establishing air superiority over a segment of the Channel long enough for a small bridgehead to be captured on the other side. (The prize was so enormous that, granted it could be seized, the cost was irrelevant and could soon be made good in the ensuing months of peace.) In view of the prevailing British weakness in every regard, it is a virtual certainty that once a foothold had been seized it would have been impossible to prevent its expansion; and once the follow-up troops started to flow through that widening bridgehead, victory must have been assured. Some argue that this was impossible. Some of great authority argued at the time that the Russians would collapse in a few weeks! If ever there was a situation which challenged a self-styled warlord to prove that "who dares, wins," this was it. It is scarcely to be supposed that Alexander or Genghis Khan or Marlborough would have hovered on the brink, "letting 'I dare not' wait upon 'I would.' " Slim's destruction of the Japanese army on the Irrawaddy in 1945 was a far more hazardous enterprise. And every week that passed after the evacuation from Dunkirk enabled the British (particularly fighter command) to increase their frail strength. The time to act was *immediately*. As a result of this major mistake Hitler, in the end, found that he had to turn to the east, leaving behind him a fortress island which would become an aircraft carrier for the Anglo-American bomber commands and a launching pad, in 1944, for D-Day.

As is usual, error was compounded by error. Hitler was in a curious frame of mind during these months. At the back of his head, for example, there still lurked that sense of *respect* for the British which is so notable a feature of *Mein Kampf*. And then he seems to have convinced himself that an invasion might not be necessary because Churchill, like a sensible statesman, would understand the realities of the situation and be prepared to open discussions for a peace treaty on what, in Hitler's view, would be "generous terms," though whether Churchill would have thought them generous is another matter.

But the most extraordinary evidence of his ambivalent state of mind during the summer of 1940 is that the British had hardly completed their evacuation before Hitler started to disband the Wehrmacht: indeed, even before the rump of the French army west of the Somme had been finished off, Hitler was discussing with von Brauchitsch a new and reduced organization for the "peacetime" German army. His initial proposals were so radical that von Brauchitsch had to exercise all his skill to inject some common sense. Even so, on July 13 he was instructed by Hitler to disband seventeen divisions and to send on leave the troops of another eighteen, on condition that they found work in industry or agriculture. What makes this decision even more extraordinary is the fact that already the Soviet Union, by annexing the Baltic States, was causing concern, and in July a whole German army, the 18th, was transferred from France to the Russian front. This seems a strange time to demobilize!

Hitler's uncertainty is best revealed by a study of the process whereby the plan for an invasion of Britain, Operation Sea-Lion, developed after a slow start from a notion into an operational proposition. An examination of the various stages whereby Sea-Lion materialized (up to October 12, 1940, when the operation was finally postponed at least until the following spring) shows Hitler, as it were, moving forward with mincing steps. At first we have a passing reference in conversation.* Then, and only gradually, Sea-Lion begins to enter into documents and directives until, for instance, on July 17 the diary of the naval operations directorate records: "It appears that OKH, which a short time ago strongly opposed such an operation, has now put aside all its doubts and regards the operation as entirely practicable." Yet though that was true of OKH (because of the three services only the army believed in Sea-Lion), Hitler himself still continued to issue *caveats* and to insist on conditions. In fact, throughout the whole of the Battle of Britain and the planning of Sea-Lion, Hitler never specifically committed himself to a directive authorizing action without inserting some qualification. This too looks like the performance of a warlord who cannot make up his mind on a vital issue; who is not prepared, in fact, to decide to dare. Thoreau once observed: "There is nothing so strong as an idea whose time has come." There is no one more successful than a military commander who is percipient enough to note when that time has arrived—and to strike.

And error continued to be compounded by error. Apart from the possibility of invading or ignoring the British Isles after the Dunkirk evacuation, there were two other options open to Hitler either of which, if it had been implemented with maximum energy, would have produced results of an enormously important, if not necessarily decisive, character. In other words, Hitler had the option of bottling up either or both of the entrances to the Mediterranean. Put simply, that meant either Gibraltar or Suez. Bearing in mind the enormous commitment of the British and Commonwealth forces to the Middle East base, and the territories on which influence could be exerted from Cairo, it is easy to see that the thought of either Suez or Gibraltar in German hands was unthinkable.

Each of these options was, in fact, carefully examined, and in each

* It was too late. If Hitler had been capable of long-term strategic planning, a skeleton scheme for Sea-Lion would have existed before the Germans crossed the Meuse.

case action to a lesser or greater degree was taken, but in Hitler's usual way indecision, delay, and an insufficient involvement of his forces meant that the vital moment was lost. Gibraltar, of course, was never captured, and the nearest that Rommel got to Suez at the very peak of his success was somewhere in the desert wilderness to the west of Alexandria and Cairo.

The "general reader," and most students of Hitler, hardly realize for how long and with what intensity the problem of Gibraltar was scrutinized. In the summer of 1940 Hitler was already issuing instructions for German troops to be earmarked for a campaign in Spain. This was the realization of an idea actually proposed as far back as June by Guderian, who requested at that time that the French armistice might be deferred so that he could rush with a couple of *Panzer* divisions across Spain, seize the Straits and cross into French North Africa. Jodl again, on August 13, had proposed the capture of Gibraltar and Suez as alternatives to Sea-Lion. Throughout all that summer Admiral Raeder was constantly seeking to impress the Führer with the vital significance of the Mediterranean, and his arguments, as has been seen, did not fall on deaf ears. In the methodical German way, volition soon began to be transformed into an operational plan. Admiral Canaris, the head of the Abwehr, had carried out an intelligence mission in Spain during July, and as the result of this, and the information he acquired about the defenses of the rock, a draft plan had already been approved by Hitler toward the end of August. By November we are dealing with specifics. The assault force, under the command of 49 Corps, was to consist of the Gebirgsjäger-Regiment No. 98 and the motorized infantry regiment Grossdeutschland.

A great weight of artillery was to be used. It is wholly characteristic of Hitler, the corporal who tried to be a warlord, and thus could never detach his mind from petty detail, that his personal map had to be marked with every British battery and defense position, and he required to be informed about the exact weight of mortar or artillery ammunition which it was intended to use against each individual position!

At the beginning of December all seemed to be going well, and the efficient and much-favored General von Reichenau had been put in charge of the Gibraltar operation, while three divisions were ready for the occupation of Portugal, and ten Gruppen (mainly dive bombers) were nominated for Felix (as the plan was called) under one of the best of the Luftwaffe commanders, von Richthofen, who had distinguished himself with his dive-bombing squadrons on the Channel coast during the Battle of Britain and the subsequent melee.*

But then disaster struck. On December 7, 1940, General Franco refused to cooperate and allow the campaign to proceed, his argument being that Spain drew too many of her vital supplies from Great Britain and the United States. Felix died instantly.

Once again, therefore, we have to ask questions about Hitler's ability, as a man who has set out to establish by conquest a greater German empire, to live according to the principle of "who dares, wins." For what were the considerations in his mind when he meekly accepted this rebuff? First, of course, he had been involved with Franco in a game of poker where the caudillo held a weak hand but was the master of the bluff. Secondly, there were relations with Vichy France to be considered, and the possibility of French North Africa turning into a nuisance. But the Great Conqueror is usually concerned with the politics of force and from that point of view Hitler held all the top cards. In spite of any warnings that might have been derived from the Peninsular War and the Spanish Civil War, there can be no doubt that in December, 1940, the divisions available to Hitler, many of them now battle-trained in Poland or Norway or France, constituted a force which Spain was quite incapable of matching. It is certainly not unreasonable to argue that if Hitler had once again exercised that famous Will and ordered his generals to smash their way through Spain, and then to capture a Gibraltar whose defenses (particularly, for instance, in antiaircraft) were no more than indifferent, he could have obtained at a relatively easy cost what Guderian had proposed: he could have closed the Atlantic entry into the Mediterranean Sea. If one recalls that this was just the time when O'Connor's offensive was thrusting westward along the African shores, and would shortly conclude by eliminating the imperial presence of the Italians, one sees from this single example—and there are many other obvious ones—what profits would have accrued if Hitler had not, in a throw-away line, dismissed his negotiations with Franco as being like a visit to the dentist, and had acted with the full brutality of which he and his commanders were capable.

The "average" reader will be equally surprised to realize that the attention paid to the problems of a German presence in North Africa

* It was the move of von Richthofen to the east in the spring of 1941 that provided the British with one of the most conclusive pieces of evidence about the coming offensive on the Russian front.

was even more extensive and prolonged than investigations into the possibility of capturing Gibraltar. Suez indeed came late into those considerations, but in the end it was Suez that dominated. In *Mein Kampf,* by contrast, the concept of colonialism is severely restricted to areas in east Europe, partly on the grounds that territory elsewhere had already been occupied by the other powers, but also because for Hitler at that time, characteristically, colonialism meant "the acquisition of territories suitable for German settlement after the expulsion, extermination or enslavement of the local population." There was not much place for Suez within such a concept. During the 1920s and early 1930s, therefore, neither Hitler nor the Nazi agencies spent much time looking overseas.

The embryonic development of a new phase occurred in 1934, when the Colonial Policy Office of the Nazi party was established under the leadership of Franz von Epp. Though Epp's authority later waned, and though he was already at loggerheads with Himmler and Heydrich, he was still a person of substance and standing within the party, as his appointment suggests. After an outstanding war career he had led a Freikorps in Munich in 1919 noted for its brutality and, in fact, had both been one of Hitler's earliest employers (as an informer) and had raised the 60,000 marks required to convert the *Völkischer Beobachter* into a Nazi organ. Thereafter he had given steady support to the Nazis and, shortly after his new appointment, Hitler granted him the prestigious post of the master of the hunt in Bavaria, promoting him to general in the following year. Thus there was a good deal of steam behind the Colonial Policy Office, at least in its early days.

By the end of December, 1938, Hitler's own policy was shifting. (The 69th Infantry Regiment in Hamburg had already been earmarked for colonial service.) Though the policy now becomes more active, it is still, on the whole, concentrated on Germany's own former colonies in West Africa and the Pacific. The defeat of Belgium in 1940 seemed to offer other opportunities—in the Congo. But all this time Epp's policy office was functioning with that mad intensity only conceivable in a German bureaucratic institution which has been given a directive to fulfill. Colonial officers, administrators and experts in tropical diseases were being assembled. Training pamphlets and the requisite maps were in preparation. It is perhaps only in Germany that at this early stage punctilious consideration should have been given to proper rates of pay and the correct fashion in which to run a post office!

But all these dreams, whether wild or feasible, were wrecked by the very country which had deterred Hitler from thinking seriously about the Central Mediterranean—Italy. France and Spain had made him distance himself from ideas about French North Africa, Morocco, etc., but it was the close relationship with Italy which prevented him from casting his eyes on Tripoli or Cyrenaica. This reservation on his part was another major mistake. He should have moved across the Mediterranean swiftly and ruthlessly in 1940. Only a handful of divisions would have been necessary. We know that until the end of the year Mussolini sought to keep German troops out of North Africa—except dive bombers, reckoning that he could get to Cairo alone. But with a clear mind about priorities, and an "iron will," Hitler was capable of browbeating Mussolini, if he so wished. The fact is that, Raeder or no Raeder, he did not perceive the strategic necessity until early 1941, when the Italians were crumbling before O'Connor's offensive and it was too late. How often does that bell ring over Hitler the great decision-maker, and how often does it prove to be the source of his mistake—too late!

The crisis point came at the turn of the year. It then became clear that instead of Mussolini driving the British out of North Africa, as had been his summer intention, he was in danger of losing his own great empire—those vast acres of Cyrenaica and Tripolitania to whose colonization and cultivation he had devoted such effort and in which he took such pride. Hitler was caught in a trap. The collapse of the Duce, his Axis partner, was unthinkable. Mere prestige forbade it. And so it was that to a portion of the continent which had not been specially studied by Ritter von Epp and his hardworking staff, and for which no thoughtful military arrangements had been made, Hitler was impelled in February, 1941, to send over the first elements of the Afrika Korps under his tried and trusted General Rommel.

We notice immediately, however, the consequences of Hitler's initial mistake in delaying a thrust across to Africa at the earliest possible moment in 1940, when alternative preoccupations were fewer. For Rommel's brilliant initial achievements against an exhausted and (at that time) incompetent British spearhead disguised the fact that he had been spared, parsimoniously, no more than a unit of *about brigade strength*. The critical moment had passed, or so it seemed in Berlin. It was not, in fact, until the summer that the Afrika Korps filled out to its restricted quota of two armored divisions, the 15th and the 21st. Rommel arrived a starveling; a starveling he remained.

Within these facts is concealed the whole future history of the German forces in North Africa. Thereafter Hitler and OKH would never spare them enough troops or supplies to carry out effectively the mission on which they had been sent—OKH because it viewed with cynicism the "African adventure," and Hitler because, though he had once tentatively committed himself, he always found reasons for withholding any significant support. Nothing better illustrates Rommel's continuing poverty than the signals which poured back from his HQ right up to the end in Africa, demanding reinforcements of tanks, and fuel, and men: these were regularly intercepted and deciphered at Bletchley Park, and thus provided Churchill and his commanders in the field with an extraordinarily vivid picture of the straits to which their enemy was being reduced.

It is true that by his cavalier brilliance Rommel struck far and deep toward the east. As the British well knew at the time, however, with every mile he advanced he was extending his lines of communication, and his perennial shortage of supplies diminished in practice the successes he so frequently achieved in battle. For this reason, it has even been doubted whether during his furthest advance to the "gates of Alexandria" in the summer of 1942 he could have sustained his momentum, as his supplies of fuel and ammunition dribbled away and his few remaining tanks continued to be eliminated—swiftly reported, by the way, to Auchinleck from Bletchley Park.

All these considerations derive from Hitler's failure of vision. In effect he thought neither Gibraltar nor Suez worth an effort which would have needed to be substantial, but not supreme. (Once again one must emphasize the percipience of Admiral Raeder in grasping the strategic value of the Mediterranean.) That lack of insight was exhibited uniquely in the summer of 1942 when, after Rommel had captured Tobruk, the question was, should he advance or should Malta be captured first. There was an Italo-German debate about Malta. Hitler could certainly have forced the issue, and there is a genuine possibility that, granted the weak British situation at the time, the island could have been captured or at least effectively neutralized during a critical period in the desert war. The loss of Malta would have been a blow to the British on an immeasurable scale. Destruction of the trans-Mediterranean convoys, which were Rommel's lifeline, would have become virtually impossible. Instantly Hitler could have reversed the strategic situation in the eastern Mediterranean. He failed to seize the opportunity. In his defense it will always be argued that the foreground of his mind was filled with an even greater commitment—Barbarossa, the invasion of Russia.

Of the two greatest mistakes committed by Hitler during the war—the invasion of Russia and the unnecessary declaration of war on the United States—it is difficult to decide which was the more disastrous since the relevant circumstances were so different. By engaging the Americans it is plain that he was responsible for his own *coup de grâce* and that he created a situation from which it was impossible to extricate himself (granted an Allied victory in the Battle of the Atlantic).*

But the Russian campaign is, or could have been, a very different proposition and though it was ruined by Hitler's own strategic decisions—by decisions taken even *before* the campaign was launched—the idea of Operation Barbarossa should not be too quickly or too contemptuously dismissed. Had the cards been played differently, Hitler might have been the Napoleon who marched beyond Moscow.† Such, it should be remembered, was the judgment *at the time* of wise and experienced soldiers on the Allied side. Both the British and the American Chiefs of Staff expected a Russian collapse. The view of the CIGS, General Dill, as recorded in his *Memoirs* by General Ismay, was that "the Germans would go through them like a hot knife through butter."

Why, therefore, were neither Hitler's hopes nor the fears of the Anglo-Americans fulfilled? The ultimate German failure, so unexpected by foreign observers, and, for that matter, by Stalin himself, who for the first few days of defeat kept a low profile to conceal his panic, was built into the Barbarossa plan itself on Hitler's personal instructions. The reason why events did not proceed in the manner or at the decisive speed anticipated was that the Führer's modifications flew in the face of all sound staff thinking, and if there was one feature of the German military machine which all other generals respected, and therefore assumed would be applied in planning, it was its meticulous staff procedures. How this deviation from the probable occurred can best be understood by following the Barbarossa concept from its earliest presentation as a practical act of war (as opposed to a theoretical desideratum in *Mein Kampf*).

* An important qualification which can more easily be made with hindsight. For a period in the spring of 1943 the Admiralty is on record as admitting a sense of despair about sustaining the Atlantic convoy routes. Then, of course, there came Dönitz's sudden astonishing admission that his U-boats had lost the battle.

† Post-war Russian revisionism has claimed, of course, that any such ideas were mere propaganda and that anyway, had the Germans thrust on past Moscow, the millions Stalin still controlled would have been unconquerable. But millions of what? A *levèe en masse*? Perhaps General Winter would have saved the day: but the case is arguable and not self-evident.

Barbarossa actually started its life as Fritz (in OKW) and Otto (in OKH). The first declaration of intent is to be found in Halder's diary, July 22, 1940, in which he records various vague aims on Hitler's part: "To defeat the Russian army, or at least to occupy as much Russian soil as is necessary to protect Berlin from air attack, it is desired to establish our own positions so far to the east that our own Air Force can destroy the most important areas of Russia." As this was the beginning of a series of discussions and declarations which indicated Russia as the next main target, Halder at OKH sensibly handed over to General Erich Marcks (the chief of staff to 18th Army) the personal function of preparing a plan for an assault on the Soviet Union—much as, in 1943, General Morgan (as chief of staff to the Allied Supreme Commander) was instructed to prepare a program for the Allied invasion of Europe. The Marcks plan, produced early in August, naturally covered many points, but its essence lay in his opening definition of the objective of the operation. In this he correctly made clear that the main centers of the Russian war economy, which provided the natural targets, lay down in the Ukraine, around Leningrad, and in the Moscow region. But, he robustly concluded, *"Of these areas, Moscow contains the economic, political and spiritual centre of the U.S.S.R. Its capture would destroy the coordination of the Russian State."* Broadly accepted by the German General Staff in an expanded form, the scenario was tried out in several war games between November 28 and December 3.* It is noteworthy that Halder's comment was that the advance of the flank army groups "would depend on the progress of the general offensive *against Moscow*." All three army groups involved carried out independent studies, each of which, in one form or another, emphasized the necessity for the primary strike at Moscow. It was thus with a sense of professional solidarity that on December 5 von Brauchitsch and Halder appeared before the Führer to present the great plan.

But Hitler, using the old trick of setting two people to do one person's job and then playing off one person against another, had already made his private arrangements. Using his power over OKW, he had ordered Jodl to undertake a completely separate and secret operational study, which Jodl in turn delegated to Baron von Lossberg. The von Lossberg

* It is a remarkable fact that during the games much thought was given to the problems of sustaining 3,500,000 men and 500,000 horses far from home in a terrain short of roads and railways, and yet little if any thought was given to the contingent possibility of having not only to sustain such a force but also to fight with it in *winter* conditions.

plan has been described as "virtually the plan on which Germany went to war." The core of his proposition was that not Moscow but the Smolensk area, some 200 miles to the west, should indeed be a target, but that further developments must depend *critically* on what happened on the flanks. It is curious that Hitler should not have been attracted by the prestige and propaganda value of a conquest of the capital city, but for a variety of reasons, some obscure, he seems to have felt no great passion in this regard. With the welcome Lossberg plan in his hands, therefore, he gave short shrift to the unfortunate generals when on that December day they presented to him confidently an alternative scheme. Indeed, after some pungent objections he ended, according to Halder's diary, *"Moscow is of no great importance."**

Walter Warlimont summarized the situation acidly: "So, with a stroke of the pen, a new concept of the main lines of the campaign against Russia was substituted for that which the OKH had worked out as a result of months of painstaking examination and crosschecking from all angles by the best military brains available." From now on, nevertheless, planning by the obedient Generalität went ahead on these lines, and from December 18 onward, as if to underline the magnitude of Hitler's conception, he altered the code name for the first time to Barbarossa. This was the actual day on which he signed Directive 21, Fall Barbarossa, which set out the whole business at interminable length.

> In the body of the directive could be traced the hand of Hitler, wearing in turn his many hats, that of industrialist and economist, of Commander-in-Chief of all armed services, of commander of army formations down to corps (he discussed the use of divisions in the Rovaniemi area) and even of Hitler the airman as he instructed the *Luftwaffe* how to deal with river bridges. *The directive thus contained a large number of disconnected objectives with priority given to none*. Hitler was about to send the German army into the Soviet Union, on a four-year will-o'-the-wisp chase after seaports, cities, oil, corn, coal, nickel, manganese and iron ore.[3]

A staff office's nightmare. It is unlikely that when the British chief of the Imperial General Staff registered his view that the Germans

* This should not be confused with Eisenhower's unwillingness to move on Berlin in 1945. He considered the city unimportant as a military objective. But, as he informed General Marshall, he was perfectly prepared to move if instructed by his superiors that there were overriding political considerations. Moscow's political significance is as obvious now as it should have been then.

would go through the Russians like a hot knife through butter, he conceived for a moment that their instructions would comprise such a miscellany, or be ruined by so many self-contradictions!

Hitler's own wayward and self-indulgent appetite was enough in itself to create the catastrophe called Barbarossa. It should be noted, however, that few enterprises so grandiose in conception can have been launched on so meager a basis of intelligence. Of course Hitler thought of intelligence as an "airy nothing"; of course he delighted in playing off one source against another (as in the case, for instance, of the Abwehr and the SS). But in at least one respect, that of his own embassy in Moscow, he cannot be exculpated. His liberal but objective and conscientious representative Count von Schulenburg made numerous attempts to convey the true facts to Hitler. His efforts were rewarded by the response to a visit he made to Berlin on April 26, at a time when he and his colleagues felt that the hour was already almost past midnight. After von Schulenburg had presented a formal memorandum and then enlarged upon it, the Führer simply rose, put the document into a drawer of his desk and, having shaken hands, said, "Thank you, this was extremely interesting." Hitler's other routine source of information, *Fremde Heere Ost* (Foreign Armies, East), the Military Intelligence Division responsible for the Russian front, was so limited in its range and competence (unlike the later days under Gehlen) that all its work was scarcely worth more than a few Boy Scout patrols.

The German army attacked with knowledge of little more than the enemy troops papering the frontier line. They were woefully ignorant about Russian armor, and the unexpected appearance on the battle front at an early date of the T34 and KV1 was the result of a myopia whose consequences are inestimable. The General Staff had also failed badly in its estimate of the speed and scope of Russian mobilization following a sudden blow—a vitally important factor. Hitler expected to wipe out all the enemy army groups at high speed. But suppose there were a hitch? The possibility, moreover, of transferring the troops on the Siberian front is a factor that seems to have been hardly weighed.

All these failures, which directly or indirectly contributed to the ultimate breakdown of Barbarossa, are sometimes claimed to be irrelevant compared with the effect of Hitler's preliminary invasion of the Balkans. But from the elaborate investigations which have been carried out there seems little question that the delay imposed on Barbarossa's D-Day (and there was a delay, for sure) occurred because spring came slowly up that way in 1941. The delay in drying out the terrain was itself a sufficient factor, bearing in mind that the German transport was largely by truck or horse-drawn, and the tracked supply vehicles, for which Guderian had pleaded as the essential ancillary of an armored thrust, had not been provided. The Balkan divisions (which had not been much hurt) certainly required a period of maintenance and replacement. But to dwell on this point is to miss the central feature of what went wrong in the operation. There were plenty of divisions in the opening phase to carve their way through a surprised and ill-trained opposition. It was after the second stage of Hitler's strategy had been applied, and his forces sprawled over European Russia from Leningrad to the Ukraine, that reinforcing divisions, more tanks, more men, more guns began to be desperately needed.

It mattered little, therefore, that for this great operation the order of battle was not significantly larger than it had been in the summer of 1940. (September 1, 1940, 3,420 tanks: June 1, 1941, 4,198 operationally serviceable.) On Hitler's map, as usual, the picture was far more impressive, because to produce more notional equipment levels divisions had been watered down, so that the *Panzer* division of May, 1940, with its 300 tanks now possessed, on average, less than 200. The antediluvian Marks 1 and 2 had indeed been reduced, yet for this modern, hard-hitting, far-reaching campaign 1,156 tanks were still of the two early Marks, while 772 were of Czech origin. For all the efforts of the armaments industry, only some 1,400 of the up-to-date Marks 3 and 4 had been provided, and these, to the Germans' astonishment, would soon prove inadequate opponents against the latest Russian armor. As to transport, it need only be observed that horse and vehicle were almost exactly equal: 600,000 trucks, etc., and 625,000 horses, many of them hauling the hastily produced country carts of Poland.

What must now be considered, however, is the fact that instead of minutely assessing these multifarious technical deficiencies (which would have existed whatever the plan employed in June, 1941) there is a different theme for argument. If Hitler had not radically modified the initial, carefully calculated staff plan for Barbarossa, and had followed the classic military principle of concentrating upon the main objective, Moscow, then perhaps before the winter shattered all hopes of an early defeat of Russia, Russia might in fact have sustained an early defeat or, Stalin having lost his nerve, might at least have been in process of submitting proposals for an armistice. A short survey of the main developments soon discloses how a real possibility was converted into a chimera.

At 3:30 on the morning of June 22, 1941, as trains still rumbled westward with their loads of oil and corn to fulfill their obligations under the Russo-German Pact, 150 Soviet divisions took the shock of the Barbarossa assault. Six weeks later, in early August, the campaign had reached a point of balance that may be described as the ending of the first phase. This, therefore, is a good point at which to examine the implications of the opening rounds of Barbarossa; and the first significance is that one should be using phrases like "point of balance" and "first phase" about an operation whose initial effect was to be that of a whirlwind! Hitler himself was satisfied as early as July 4 that the war was over, to all intents and purposes. How right it was, he said, that "we smashed the Russian armor and air forces right at the beginning." But nothing had been "smashed." In various great encirclements the Russians had indeed already lost 1,250,000 men. The Germans, for their part, had lost 15% of their troops (200,000) and a quarter of their armor (863 tanks). The Germans were still a potent force, and the Russians were severely wounded, but none could say that the war was over.

The central question was still there, as it had always been: should a drive be launched directly on Moscow? A detailed study of events during the next few weeks—order and counterorder and disorder, marching and countermarching, generals quarreling with generals, and senior officers even standing up to Hitler—shows the danger of embarking on a great enterprise without the most precise clarification of objectives, both immediate and long-term. For the truth is that now the great army machine simply did not know what to do. The more serious and independent generals were all for making straight for Moscow. But as usual Hitler veered, sometimes wanting more effort to be made against Leningrad, sometimes turning his eye to the corn and the oil of the south, the industries of the Donets basin, the Crimea—"that aircraft carrier against our Roumanian oilfields"—and even the far reaches of the Caucasus. From time to time he would also tinker with the idea of Moscow, but lazily and without appetite. Finally, after an infinity of discussion and changes of mood, he made up his mind. On August 12 his supplement to Directive No. 34 set out the new scheme. In the north, proceed as usual. In the south, drive for the Crimea, the Donets and Kharkov. But in the center no more was proposed than a forward move which might enable the capital to be cut off but not entered. "The object of operations must then be to deprive the enemy, before the coming winter, of his government, armaments and traffic centers *around* Moscow, and thus prevent the rebuilding of his defeated forces and the orderly working of government control."

But it was hopeless. By October 14, 673,000 prisoners had been taken, 1,242 tanks and 5,412 guns: but it was not enough. The Germans had made the mistake the British made at Passchendaele: they had forgotten the weather. Conditions rapidly became subhuman, supply systems failed and it was more a question of surviving than of fighting.

> Gradually the most simple necessities of life disappeared, razorblades, soap, toothpaste, shoe repairing materials, needles and thread. Even in September, and before the onset of winter, there was incessant rain and a cold north-east wind, so that every night brought with it the scramble for shelter, squalid and bug-ridden though this usually was. When this could not be found the troops plumbed the very depths of wretchedness. The rain, cold and lack of rest increased sickness that, in normal circumstances, would have warranted admission to hospital; but the sick had to march with the column over distances of up to twenty-five miles a day, since there was no transport to carry them and they could not be left behind in the wild bandit-infested forests. The regulation boots, the *Kommissstiefel,* were falling to pieces. All ranks were filthy and bearded, with dirty, rotting and verminous underclothing; typhus was shortly to follow.[4]

For leaders with a conscience the predicament was appalling, as Guderian wrote to his wife in November. "The icy cold, the lack of shelter, the shortage of clothing, the heavy losses of men and equipment, the wretched state of our fuel supplies, all this makes the duties of a commander a misery and the longer it goes on the more I am crushed by the responsibility which I have to bear." A *Panzer* general might well feel concerned, for Guderian also recorded: "Ice was causing a lot of trouble since the calks for the tanks had not yet arrived. The cold made the telescopic sights useless: the salve which was supposed to prevent this also had not arrived. In order to start the engines of the tanks, fires had to be lit beneath them, fuel was freezing on occasions and the oil became viscous."

As replacements became impossible and casualties mounted, OKH took the inevitable decision. On December 5 the attack was called off. The good sense of the decision did not impress itself on Hitler who, according to Halder, "refuses to take any account of comparative figures of strengths. To him our superiority is proved by the numbers of prisoners taken." Yet in spite of his insistence that the battle should continue, by December 8 he too accepted the truth, with his face-saving Directive No. 39: "The severe winter weather which has come surprisingly early on the east and the consequent difficulties in bringing up supplies, compel us to abandon immediately all major offensive operations and go over to the defensive." Thus on the 168th day of Barbarossa the objective which ought to have been gained, had all forces been concentrated on Moscow from the start with single-minded intent, had to be at least temporarily abandoned. It is scarcely necessary to add that the year's remaining question was resolved in a way wholly characteristic of the Führer. He brought his Will to bear, and flatly refused to allow withdrawal into more comfortable winter positions. His army fought and froze where it stood.

> Only he who saw the endless expanse of Russian snow during this winter of our misery, and felt the icy wind that blew across it, burying in snow every object in its path; who drove for hour after hour through no-man's land only at last to find too thin shelter with insufficiently clothed, half-starved men; and who also saw by contrast the well-fed, warmly clad and fresh Siberians fully equipped for winter fighting—only a man who knew all that can truly judge the events which now occurred.[5]

8

THE SUPREMO

They were fighting a war that they did not want under a Commander-in-Chief who did not trust them and whom they themselves did not fully trust, by methods contrary to their experience and accepted views, with troops and police that were not completely under their control.

—COLONEL-GENERAL JODL, OF HIS FELLOW GENERALS

"Anyone can do the little job of directing operations in war," Hitler told Halder in December, 1941. "The task of the Commander-in-Chief is to educate the Army to be National Socialist. I do not know any Army general who can do this as I want it done. I have therefore decided to take over command of the Army myself." He had, in fact, just sacked—on the 19th—an exhausted and dispirited Brauchitsch and, as supreme commander, had assumed personal responsibility for OKH as well as OKW, keeping Halder as the army chief of staff but switching to Keitel at OKW the administrative control of all the forces which OKH had so far directed. During December and early January, moreover, he made a clean sweep of "difficult" generals—von Rundstedt, von Bock, von

Leeb, Guderian, Hoepner and over thirty more senior officers with high commands in the field. Von Reichenau departed, too, dying of a heart attack on January 17. "Thus, in mid-December Hitler concluded a process which began in early 1938 . . . The corporal of the First World War had, indeed, become the warlord of the Second."[1]

It was a fatal apotheosis, a major mistake which encapsulated many of Hitler's weakest features—his grotesque overconfidence in regard to his mastery of the art and science of war; his resentment of "opposition" by subordinates, even when the case they argued was disinterested and correct; his assumption that willpower and ideological fervor counted for more in battle than the serious judgment of highly trained staffs; the preference for toadies, who now formed a close circle around him at his headquarters in east Prussia and, with their uncritical flattery, magnified his self-esteem.* By his assumption of the supreme command, moreover, he found it possible to play at the highest level the game on which he had always relied in his conduct of affairs, that of divide and rule. By duplicating responsibilities between OKH and OKW he was able to set one off against the other even more maliciously than in the past, and from now on every German battle commander knew that there was only one real arbiter and only one source of power—the Führer. The consequence was stultifying, and well epitomized later in the war by von Rundstedt when he complained that he could not even change a sentry without Hitler's permission. Uncontrolled and uncontrollable, the corporal who claimed to have read Clausewitz (but had only skimmed the surface) drove Germany forward on a course which, from the beginning of 1942 to the end of the war, steadily expelled her troops from every occupied territory and terminated where the whole grandiose process had begun—in besieged Berlin.

It was appropriate that Russia should have been the theater in which Hitler felt the compulsion to grasp every rein in his own hand, for it was in Russia, if anywhere, that circumstances demanded from him the exercise of the most exquisite military skills. It is in the east that his performance, and massive failure, as a *feldherr* must be most critically assessed, since this was the decisive point—that decisive point at which, according to all the ancient principles of war, one's maximum force must be concentrated and effectively exerted. It was in Russia that far more German divisions were continuously assembled

* From July, 1942, Hitler had an advance command post at Vinnitsa in the Ukraine.

throughout the war than on any other front: Russia which was the prime objective of Hitler's imperial ambitions: and Russia which, for historical, ideological and geopolitical reasons, offered the most menacing threat to the Nazi New Order. Here was the enormous cockpit within which mass armies, the embodiment of the national wills, must inevitably slug it out to a final conclusion. There is a real sense in which the campaigns in the east were, for Hitler, the equivalent of the western front in the First World War—the one region where defeat was inadmissible and victory carried the future in its hands.

Nevertheless, Hitler, like Roosevelt (but unlike Churchill), was more than a commander-in-chief—he was also the political head of state.* And it may well be argued, as many have done, that in Russia Hitler's most profound mistakes were not military (massive and manifold though these may have been) but political and sociological. We shall note, in due course, such terrible disasters as Stalingrad and Kursk, but their effects are identifiable and quantifiable. It is impossible to quantify the loss sustained by Hitler through his willful failure to win "the hearts and minds" of the inhabitants of many of the vast areas of the USSR which his armies overran. Yet there was the possibility of a bloodless victory here which was his for the taking.

> The reception we received from civilians was astonishingly cordial. Entering the villages we were greeted as liberators. Except for officials of the Communist Party, practically nobody fled. The Soviet government's efforts to evacuate the population from the areas under the German threat were widely obstructed and generally a failure. The only areas in which the Soviet government succeeded in evacuating the machinery and personnel of industrial plants were all at a considerable distance from the front lines. Nor did the peasants heed the orders of the Soviet government to destroy the harvest and all grain reserves, or to drive off their cattle. Stalin's order to leave the occupied territories to the German invaders as scorched earth was viewed by the peasantry as an act of despair and only served to intensify their hatred of the dictator. The local population showed genuine kindness towards the German troops and pinned great hopes on our arrival. Everywhere we went we were greeted with bread and salt, the traditional Slav symbols of hospitality.

This account by a young German cavalry officer of his experiences during the early advance can be duplicated over and over again. Nor

* Stalin also doubled the role, though it was not until August, 1941, that he became commander-in-chief.

was the opportunity so proffered merely the result of the first Blitzkrieg assault. As Hitler with an insensate optimism drove his right wing farther and farther eastward,* beyond the Crimea to the Caucasus and onward, as he hoped, to Turkey, to the oilfields, to the canal and even to a linkup with Japan, he was in fact "liberating" from Stalin's oppression precisely those areas and nationalities most likely to hand over to him their hearts and minds—the Ukrainians, the Caucasians, the Cossacks, the Tartars, peoples fired by centuries of resentment against their Russian masters.† All that was necessary was a soft hand and a soft word.

Instead they got the SS. The activities of the special annihilation squads or Einsatzgruppen had, of course, started immediately in Poland in 1939, when three of the Death's Head units which had previously guarded concentration camps in Germany were switched to more positive efforts, the torture or murder of Polish Jews, intellectuals, aristocrats, priests, businessmen, etc. It is significant that their commander, Eicke, the "higher SS leader for the conquered regions of Poland," operated during the campaign from Hitler's private headquarters train. This is not the place to elaborate on that dreadful story which even put to shame some German generals like Blaskowitz. One may simply point out, with an absolutely clinical detachment, that in the severely practical terms of the politics of force Hitler's tortuous mind may have seen a defensible case for eliminating any possible elements of resistance in Poland, since that proud people, unforgiving and unforgetting, could never conceivably be regarded as equals within the Nazi New Order. But this was certainly not the case in, say, the Ukraine. It could easily have been seen not to be the case even before Barbarossa was launched. This misperception of Hitler's must count as one of his most obtuse political errors. Beside it Churchill's obstinate refusal, throughout the war, to allow any progress in India's desire for self-determination shrivels into insignificance.

The result of Hitler's decision to intimidate and extirpate rather than

* A relevant document is Hitler's Directive No. 32, issued on June 11, 1941, so that forward planning could be initiated and "so that I may issue final directives before the campaign in the East is over." It envisaged the seizure of Gibraltar and the destruction of the British control of the Middle East by converging attacks from Libya through Egypt, from Bulgaria through Turkey, and from Caucasia through Iran.

† There was another common chord: anti-Semitism. It is worth recalling that in Paris in 1926 the Yiddish poet Scholam Schwartzbard assassinated Semyan Petliura, the Ukrainian leader, in revenge for the murder by Ukrainians of many thousands of Jews in pogroms during the Russian Civil War.

to attempt conciliation was disastrous. Himmler, to whom he virtually gave *carte blanche*, set as his target the elimination of 3,000,000 Slavs, and if he fell short of that objective his henchmen worked with the same inhuman efficiency as Stalin's during the great purges of the Kulaks and the Soviet military establishment. The number of Einsatzgruppen sent into Russia was in fact small; these specialists in slaughter never amounted to much more than some 3,000. But they provided a focus and an example for many like-minded agencies and executioners. Nor could the German generals be exonerated. Hitler had trapped them in advance. At the meeting in the Reich Chancellery on March 17, 1941, when he briefed them on the campaign, he announced that "the war against Russia will be such that it cannot be conducted in a knightly fashion. This struggle is a struggle of ideologies and racial differences and will have to be waged with unprecedented, unmerciful and unrelenting harshness." At the same time he gave the notorious order for the liquidation of political commissars attached to Soviet units, a breach of international law from which he specifically absolved the Wehrmacht. In May Keitel circulated the text of the order. The generals may have protested *in private*, but thereafter they went mysteriously blind.

Complaisant commanders and the fervor of the SS produced a climate of terror whose manifestations ranged from those pathetic trenches crammed with peasant corpses to the truly ostentatious battues—33,000 Jews murdered in two days at Kiev in September, 1941, for example, or 16,000 at Pinsk in 1942. (That ideological bigot, Major-General Otto Ohlendorf of the SS, whose *Einsatzgruppe D* functioned in the areas of deepest penetration down in the south, was responsible for the death of some 90,000 men, women and children. At Nuremberg he claimed that this task, "psychologically an immense burden to bear," was historically necessary as a means of acquiring *Lebensraum* for the Reich. He and three other *Einsatzgruppe* commanders were executed by hanging in Landsberg prison in June, 1951.)

Inevitably the friendship initially proffered to the Germans in the occupied territories, which they might so easily have prolonged, turned to hostility. The Russian High Command, moreover, rapidly exacerbated the situation by inserting party activists behind the enemy lines. Willingly or under duress, the peoples of the countryside turned to partisan warfare. Sometimes the party men would commit atrocities in the knowledge that savage reprisals would follow, and thus intensify the peasants' hatred for the enemy. (Communist resistance groups in

France had a similar policy.) From the first winter of the war onward, therefore, the German lines of communication, so often demolished by the weather, were further exposed to the ravages of the partisans, who were frequently brigaded into considerable units and furnished with supplies and weapons from the home front. Thus it was that the Germans, who might have had a relatively placid "sea to swim in," made for themselves a maelstrom.

But it was not only in the short term, i.e., for the duration of the war, that the Germans suffered from a political error on Hitler's part which had grave military consequences. We have to reflect on the alienation (and murder) of millions of Russians in the light of the Führer's ultimate objective, that Thousand Year Reich. How could it be expected, assuming a German victory, that the situation in the east would be other than that so mordantly described by Tacitus, *ubi solitudinem faciunt, pacem appellant*, "where they make a wilderness, they call it peace"? Earlier in the war Rosenberg and the huge staff that worked in his ministry for the East evolved an elaborate plan for fragmenting the USSR into a number of separatist states, pastoralizing them and policing the territories with a series of what must have been very lonely German outposts, akin to the guardians of the eastern marches in the olden days, the forts of the U.S. Cavalry in Red Indian territory or British garrisons on the Northwest Frontier. Hitler squashed the project, but in practice he would have been compelled, if he had achieved his aim, to maintain a system of permanent subjugation. The sum of previous history confirms that this was not a recipe for a durable empire. "Each man kills the thing he loves," wrote Oscar Wilde. Even before the gestatory period was over, Hitler destroyed any hope for the child, the Teutonic empire, whose future he had painted in such glowing colors.

Operation Barbarossa was hardly a few weeks old before Halder, who squared up to his diary with more self-assurance than when he faced his Führer, noted on July 23 that "he has decided on his objectives and sticks to them without considering what the enemy may do, or taking account of any other points of view": and again, on August 23, "In my view the situation resulting from the Führer's interference is intolerable for the Army. These individual instructions from the *Führer* produce a situation of order, counter-order and disorder and no one can be held responsible but he himself personally." It may be said that such comments were but ranging rounds for the storm of defensive fire which the generals would discharge after 1945, at Nuremberg, during their interrogations and later in their memoirs, a protective screen which was intended, when the smoke had cleared, to leave Hitler's military reputation in fragments and their own unimpaired. If only they had been left alone! But the argument cannot be sustained. Of course those hardbitten professionals would have produced better results if they had been able to exercise without interference the traditional skills of their craft, but in a final analysis it was the professionals themselves who surrendered unconditionally to their master. During the vital debate at headquarters on August 23, 1941 (over the issue of an immediate advance on Moscow), Guderian, as he noted, "saw for the first time that . . . all those present nodded in agreement with every sentence that Hitler uttered." The heads never stopped nodding, not even, except in the case of a few brave spirits, when those preparing the assassination plot of July 20, 1944, offered them the opportunity of taking decisive action. There is no escape clause for the Generalität.

Still, in essence Halder was right. Hitler's assumption of the post of commander-in-chief in December, 1941, was merely a ratification of what had existed for almost a decade—the final enabling act, which gave an institutional sanction to his dictatorial powers as a military overlord just as the earlier act had consecrated his civil domination. Whether his generals were servile or incompetent is less significant than the fact that Hitler now had what he always sought, supreme authority in every sphere. He was not daunted, but delighted: for only he had the unbreakable Will, only his heaven-sent presence could assure victory, and only he understood that the mystic force of ideology gave Germany a greater strength than all Stalin's hordes could muster. He accepted with pride those situations in which, as Halder put it, "no one can be held responsible but he himself personally." Since he alone created and master-minded them, he alone deserves to be weighed in the balance. The paradigm of all his military misjudgments is Stalingrad.

The list of specific but secondary errors which Hitler committed in the course of the Russian campaign is extensive, and from a technical point of view each would be worth studying in detail, since in combination they form a characteristic pattern of thought and behavior, a style, which (if properly understood) can be identified in his command and control of all the other theaters of war, in North Africa, in Italy, in northwest Europe. Most of the mistakes he made elsewhere he perpetrated in Russia, but on a larger scale. It is a notable fact that the considerable commanders—Marlborough, for example, Wellington, Grant, Foch, Montgomery—have a recognizable "identikit," a way of organizing their conduct of war which is personal, perceptible, distinctive. Hitler, like Napoleon, is exceptional in that while he too had a characteristic style of command, and applied it in operations on the largest scale, its ultimate by-product (unlike that of many memorable men of war) was not victory but defeat.

Those specific mistakes, though secondary, are still striking. In war, for example, time and space present multidimensional problems, nowhere more so than on the great blotting pad of Russia. Yet Hitler had no proper grasp of these parameters. He profoundly erred, too, in undertaking extensive operations on widely separated fronts with a diminishing Luftwaffe which was incapable of supporting effectively more than one front at a time, thus handing over to the Russians the initiative in the air: it was not often, at least from 1943 onward, that the Luftwaffe's front-line strength in the east rose above 2,000, whereas Soviet aircraft production had already surpassed that of Germany and at its peak had an annual output of some 40,000 planes. Then there was that constant and unpredictable shifting of emphasis from one front to another. Maintenance of the objective, a classic principle of war, was rejected by the man for whom intuition was more peremptory than rational processes. He might dazzle his sycophants, and even some of his skeptical generals, by the way that his flypaper memory retained like gum the technical details of weaponry, the strength and location of even the smallest units, the amount and types of ammunition or armor available at a particular spot, but all this was essentially cosmetic by comparison with his myopia in regard to the basic necessities and fundamental rules of war.

Nothing disheartened the intelligent among his subordinates more than his belief that Will is overriding, so that time and time again he would demand that his troops held out to the last on lines and in positions from which all military logic demanded a withdrawal. This obsession was magnified by his practice of running the war by remote control, assuming that he could assess the realities of a battle situation by studying the pins and colored markings on the maps in a command post many hundreds of miles from the scene of action. All the bitter criticism leveled at Haig and his staff for their failure to comprehend the conditions at Passchendaele are as nothing compared with the censure that Hitler merited in this regard. And it was at a critical point in the great German offensive in the spring of 1918 that Haig rode slowly down the Menin road with his lancer escort, *toward the enemy,* encouraging his shattered troops by his mere presence and calm demeanor. When, it may be asked, did the Führer ever advance to a stricken field?* On June 17, 1944, indeed, he ventured as far west as Soissons to discuss with Rundstedt and Rommel the desperate situation in Normandy, but next morning an errant V1 flying bomb fell and exploded near his headquarters. "Hitler," as Liddell Hart put it in *The Rommel Papers,* "turned straight round and made off to the Reich, leaving the Western front to its fate."

For the student of Hitler's military incapacity Stalingrad is not merely significant because, like Midway in the Pacific war, it was a turning point, the point at which psychological as well as material superiority began to swing remorselessly in the Russians' favor. It is indicative because all through the long months of 1942 which culminated, in the following February, with the surrender of a field marshal, twenty-four generals and 91,000 men, Hitler revealed one by one, and often simultaneously, every flaw in his makeup as a warlord. Neither his judgment nor his personality proved adequate for the massive strain and, indeed, their dual frailty was evident from the beginning, as Halder recorded:

> When he read a statement compiled from unimpeachable sources which showed that in 1942 Stalin would still be able to muster another one to 1¼ million men in the region north of Stalingrad and west of the Volga, and at least half a million more in the eastern Caucasus and the region to its north, and which proved moreover that the Russian output of first line tanks amounted to at least 1200 a month, Hitler flew with clenched fists and foam in the corners of his mouth at the one who was reading this statement, and forbade such idiotic nonsense.

In spite of such warnings Hitler embarked, early in 1942, on a grandiose two-pronged offensive whose initial architecture, at least, had some sort of rationale. While Bock (who had been reinstated) pressed with his Army Group B for Stalingrad and the crossings of the Volga, far to the south General List and his mobile Army Group A (their left flank shielded by Bock) were to thrust irresistibly onward

* *"La présence du général est indispensable; c'est la tête, c'est le tout d'une armée: ce n'est pas l'armée romaine qui a soumis la Gaule, mais César . . . ce n'est pas l'armée prussienne qui a défendu sept ans la Prusse contre les trois plus grandes de l'Europe, mais Frédéric le Grand";* Napoleon. Hitler constantly referred to Frederick as a model, particularly during Germany's decline, but never understood or practiced this vital aspect of his leadership.

through the Caucasus to Baku and the oilfields. Then, with intuition following intuition like a wavering flight of butterflies, Hitler disastrously changed his plan not once but twice, first switching Hoth's 4 *Panzer* Army southward from the Stalingrad front before anything substantial had been achieved there. Then, while List was still stuck and struggling in the Caucasus, Hoth was switched back to Stalingrad, where, by now, the Russians had been granted time to stiffen their defenses, although the first German onslaught had driven them into an extreme and well-recorded confusion. "This chopping and changing reminds us of D'Erlon's Reserve Corps at Waterloo, which marched and counter-marched between Ligny and Quatre Bras, unable to influence either battle." Like Napoleon, Hitler was to lose—game, set and match.

For now all the other factors came into play. Because Stalin wore a halo for his work in 1919 as a commissar in the region of the city which now bore his name, Hitler attached to its fall a personal and almost mystical significance. It became a matter of all or nothing, world domination or defeat! Yet the Volga could well have been crossed at other places and the oil of Baku was of far greater importance than a prestigious capture of Stalingrad. Then came the ritual sacking of the generals: first Bock, and then Halder. Then, after shedding List, Hitler himself took over direct command of Army Group A, though how he expected to marshal from afar its *Panzer* divisions through the mountains of the southeast passes comprehension. As well-gauged Russian counterattacks on either flank cut off and surrounded von Paulus's 6th Army outside Stalingrad two other characteristic Hitlerian traits were disclosed. First, he misjudged, once again, the capability of the Luftwaffe, and believed Göring's crazy boast that he could keep von Paulus supplied by air—in the Russian winter, with a wholly inadequate transport fleet and only the odd landing ground within the 6th Army's perimeter. The result—some 3,000 tons delivered for a loss of nearly 500 aircraft. Now the situation was irrecoverable. A relief attempt by von Manstein got within a fair distance of the beleaguered army, but the order to break out never came. Hitler's other fantasy prevailed. They would stand fast to the end and he would *will* them to victory. Instead, a historic surrender, and for the first time Germany had lost the initiative in the Second World War. Hitler's culpability is unquestionable.

It might, perhaps, seem as though the other spectacular drama for which Hitler was mainly responsible was also an exercise in initiative.

This was the great conflict at Kursk, fought out during three weeks in July, 1943—the most elaborate tank battle, so far, in the history of warfare, a battle whose meaning for the Germans may be measured mathematically. Of the 4,500 tanks and assault guns available at that date for the Wehrmacht and the SS divisions, two thirds were on the Russian front, of which no less than 70% were deployed at Kursk.

By the spring of 1943 Germany's position on the world stage was already waning. The Allies were now masters of the North African shore, the Mediterranean would soon be a freeway for their shipping, and Mussolini was looking for peace with Russia. Almost certainly, Europe's "soft underbelly" would be invaded at some point or other. In the Far East the fortunes of the Axis were also declining, for in New Guinea and the Solomons a succession of defeats by land, sea and air had set the Japanese decisively on the long road homeward. Both American and Russian industrial production were now in high gear and, for all Speer's valiant efforts, Germany would never regain her superiority in armaments. The Combined Bomber Offensive, launched by the Casablanca Conference at the beginning of the year, was about to make its inroads into German stocks of day fighters and anti-aircraft equipment, while German cities were continuously pulverized. All the elements in Hitler's personality, all his instincts and ingrained habits, demanded from him at this moment some sudden theatrical coup, some undeniable demonstration of German resilience and residual power: something, he said, that would "shine out to the world like a beacon." The setting he selected was Kursk. *Zitadelle* was the code name given to the operation, but unfortunately the citadel proved to be impregnable.

At Kursk the Russian line bulged forward invitingly, flanked as it was by two German salients jutting eastward; on the right, their positions centered on Kharkov and in the north the prong pushed out around Orel. On Hitler's map the scenario seemed to present a perfect opportunity for the maneuver first described by the great von Schlieffen as *Vernichtungsgedanke*, the battle of annihilation which leads to the total destruction of an enemy force not by direct assault but by swift, sudden, ruthless attacks on its flanks and rear, attacks which cause the enemy to be surrounded and result in that favorite German military concept, the Kesselschlacht or caldron battle. So the Führer, much encouraged by his new lackey, Zeitzler (who had replaced Halder as chief of staff), decided that von Kluge's Army Group Center and von Manstein's Army Group South should mount converging attacks on the flanks of the Kursk salient, grip it in their pincers and consummate a famous victory. His dreams (and his gnawing concern) are reflected in his Order of the Day:

> Soldiers of the *Reich*! This day you are about to take part in an offensive of such importance that the whole future of the war may depend on its outcome. More than anything else, your victory will show the whole world that resistance to the power of the German Army is hopeless.

Alas, when that order was issued in early July (for what, in the event, was Germany's last major offensive in Russia) it was already too late. Even Hitler confessed to his commanders, on July 1, that it was all a gamble. Yet he was the culprit, for only he could nominate D-Day, and he dillied and dallied so long in making up his mind that when at last his divisions were launched, the Russians were fully prepared with defenses in great depth, a million men, minefield upon minefield, massed artillery and huge quantities of armor, particularly the T34 which continued to be the best tank in the Russian theater. One of Hitler's reasons for postponing Zitadelle from May to June, and from June to July, was that his own tanks coming off the production line, the Panthers in particular, would prove decisive. But the Panthers were slow in coming and disappointing in performance, their tracks wrongly designed for the Russian terrain. (On the southern flank torrential downpours turned the battlefield into a quagmire.) Guderian (now back as inspector-general of Armor), that shrewd commander Model, von Manstein and, in the end, Zeitzler himself had little hope of success. To cap it all, Hitler's intelligence service was deficient, for nobody warned him that the Russians were not only preparing six defensive belts covered by over 3,000 tanks and 20,000 guns: they were actually so confident that they were also preparing to mount a large-scale summer offensive themselves.

By contrast, the British signal-intelligence organization at Bletchley Park provided, through its ability to read the German Enigma cipher, an astonishingly regular and detailed picture of the enemy's strength and intentions on the eastern front—by no means always complete or even accurate, but abundantly superior to anything of a comparable character that was available for Hitler and OKW. Thus the first evidence of German preparations was noted as early as March, and by the end of April deciphered intercepts had revealed the broad intention as well as the Zitadelle code name. On April 30 the gist of this information and a warning about an impending attack on the Kursk salient was passed to the Russian General Staff (without revealing the source) by the British military mission in Moscow. While it is true that thereafter the clear image presented to the chiefs of staff and the Prime Minister became somewhat blurred (it was not, for example, until July 10 that Bletchley established the outbreak of Zitadelle), nevertheless the slow development of German preparations on the ground telegraphed to the Russians in unmistakable terms the imminence and scale of what was about to happen. So they were ready, and by the end of July Stalin was able to make a public announcement (and a truthful one) that Zitadelle had been "completely frustrated." On Hitler's part vaulting ambition had been negated by dithering indecision. Once again excessive confidence in his own technical expertise had caused him to overvalue the capability of his weapons, and once again he had trampled over the doubts of his most experienced and sensible commanders. It was the old recipe for disaster, and the result was inevitable. How often the generals must have muttered to themselves, in their own formulation, Admiral Collingwood's *cri de coeur:* "I do wish Nelson would stop signalling: we all know what to do!" But the signals never stopped and they had lost, by default, the capacity to resist them.

Unlike that at Stalingrad, moreover, the overwhelming defeat at Kursk was compounded by sinister news from another main theater of war—news which signified the climacteric consequence of an equally characteristic series of vacillations and misjudgments on Hitler's part. A week after the start of Zitadelle Anglo-American troops made their first landings in Sicily. On July 13 Hitler summoned the commanders of his army groups to inform them that the Italians were a broken reed, that Sicily was doomed, that attacks on the mainland must be expected and that reinforcements must therefore be transferred from the Russian front to create new formations in Italy and the Balkans. And, indeed, within another week the Fascist Grand Council had assembled, the king had ousted Mussolini and Badoglio had put together an alternative government about which Hitler immediately observed: "Undoubtedly in their treachery they will proclaim that they will remain loyal to us. Of course they won't remain loyal . . . We'll capture all that riffraff." But in effect the Führer was now in a strategic dilemma—"between," as the Americans put it, "a rock and a hard place."

The question is, was such a trap unavoidable? It may be put in another form. Was the final signal dispatched from the headquarters of the Afrika Korps in Tunisia on May 13, 1943—"Ammunition shot off. Arms and equipment destroyed. In accordance with orders received the German Afrika Korps has fought itself into the condition where it can fight no more"—an appropriate epitaph for a venture which was doomed from the start, or was it rather an ironic comment on that bungling by Hitler which had resulted in the surrender, at an African Dunkirk, of some 230,000 Axis soldiers of whom about half were German?

With hindsight we can see that even if a reasonable proportion of those troops had been made available for Rommel in 1941 or early 1942, the period when British fortunes in the desert were at their nadir, Mussolini might have fulfilled his dream of riding on his white horse into Cairo and, more importantly, Hitler might have possessed the Mediterranean and the canal, with who knows what opportunities for further exploitation in the Levant and the Middle East. Admiral Raeder and the Navy needed no hindsight: they perceived these possibilities at the time and urged them on a stone-deaf Führer. Because of the euphoria over Alamein we forget what a *small* war was fought in the desert. We overlook too readily the difference that even one or two more good armored or motorized divisions might have made to Rommel and on what narrow margins—of men, of tanks and artillery, of aircraft and other equipment—the British always had to rely as a result of their extended communications and their far-flung commitments. Hitler never noticed that he could pick up North Africa on the cheap if he put his professionals to work with a clear directive.

If this was a blind spot which may be explained, though not excused, by pointing to his obsession with the preparation for, and execution of, Barbarossa, there is nothing to justify the mistake which he made in the summer of 1942, for the issue and its implications were clear as day. After Rommel had captured Tobruk the initial plan, endorsed by Hitler, was for him then to delay any major advance until Malta, the enfeebling ulcer in the flank of the Afrika Korps, had been eliminated. Instead Rommel, with that impetuosity which needed so firm a control, pleaded to be allowed to "press on regardless." Hitler agreed, Malta survived, and the key to Rommel's defeat at Alamein is the cutting of his lifeline—the flow of fuel and supplies across the Mediterranean—by British strike forces which could certainly have not operated with such effect if Malta's harbor and airfield had been in enemy hands. As a strategic misjudgment which was almost amateur in quality, Hitler's refusal to risk taking Malta by assault must be equated with the decision, by Eisenhower and Montgomery, to make for Arnhem before they had cleared the approaches to the port of Antwerp. In each case false hopes of a dramatic success obscured the correct military objective. These are not the errors that should be committed by a man who prides himself on his capacity as a warlord.

"I alone bear the responsibility for Stalingrad," Hitler announced to von Manstein, a cock-crow which had its origins in his belief that by forcing the army to stand fast in front of Moscow during the winter of 1941 his military genius and his willpower had been exemplified by contrast with the pusillanimity of his generals. From then on any suggestion on their part for a withdrawal or a sensible tactical readjustment of the front line produced the automatic reflex action, "No." How was it possible to conduct a campaign fruitfully when the commander-in-chief felt nothing but contempt for his subordinates? Yet by May 9, 1943, Goebbels was noting in his diary:

> He is absolutely sick of the generals. He can't imagine anything better than having nothing to do with them. His opinion of all the generals is devastating. Indeed, at times it is so caustic as to seem prejudiced or unjust, although on the whole it no doubt fits the case . . . All generals are opposed to National Socialism. All generals are reactionaries . . . He can't stand them. They have disappointed him too often.

On July 20, 1944, it might be said, there was good cause for that sense of disappointment. But long before then, along the African shores, Hitler's misanthropy in regard to his commanders and his uninhibited readiness to squander German lives in hopeless "last-ditch" actions had unfortunate consequences.

An outstanding error was his response to Rommel's despairing signal of November 2, 1942, at the tail end of Alamein, in which the man he had once applauded and presented with a field marshal's baton reported that in view of the depletion of his fuel and ammunition stocks, and the exhaustion of his troops, he was embarking on a step-by-step retreat. No sound military critic would dispute the logical necessity of this decision, but Hitler went up in flames, dispatching the famous reply which began, "With me the entire German people is watching your heroic defensive battle in Egypt . . . in your situation there can be no thought but of persevering, of yielding not one yard . . . To your troops therefore you can offer no other path than that leading to Victory or Death."

It is impossible to imagine what Hitler expected to gain by this instruction other than some Wagnerian demonstration of the German/National Socialist spirit, invincible even in its death throes. Like the Führer's own hortatory message, the instructions for all supply ships sent to Rommel during the Alamein battle had been intercepted, deciphered at Bletchley Park and reported to the British Middle East Command. Every ship, with its cargo of fuel and ammunition, had immediately been sunk by strike forces: *Prosperina* and *Tergestea* on October 26, *Luisiano* on the 28th (a loss which Rommel considered "shattering"), and *Tripolino* and *Ostia* on November 1. With his tanks and German troops decimated and the Italians disheartened, Rommel was now restricted to the uncertainties and inadequacies of air supply or the long land route from Benghazi and Tripoli, at best a gas-guzzling, vulnerable and roundabout itinerary. There was no answer but to get back as far as possible as fast as possible—"advancing westward," as Goebbel's propaganda put it. But it was just this respite that Hitler denied to the Afrika Korps.

Montgomery's failure to cut off Rommel when he finally retreated, an unpredictable failure, is another story. More relevant is the fact that it was probably during those last dark nights of despair at Alamein that Rommel's mind began to shift decisively from a general dissatisfaction with the regime to the more positive course which brought him into association, if not connivance, with the July 20 plotters, and ended with his murder, in October, 1944, by a brace of Hitler's adjutants. Rommel's alienation is a particularly striking example of the disillusion that Hitler's personal conduct of the war could breed even in the most devoted and dashing of his commanders. By contrast the British desert leaders, Wavell and Auchinleck, were both unseated by Churchill with what at the time seemed a ruthless vigor (though postwar research has justified the prime minister) but neither, in his most bitter mood of resentment, ever envisaged a clandestine retaliatory reaction.

The last retreat from Alamein coincided with the Anglo-American landings in Northwest Africa, Torch, to be followed in due course by the assaults on Sicily and the Italian mainland. It is at this point, the epicenter of the Second World War, that Hitler's capacity to "see things steadily and see them whole" is most severely called into question. During the great battles on the western front in the earlier war Marshal Foch had the endearing habit of entering some perplexed command post and asking the simple question: *"De quoi s'agit-il?"* "What's the central issue?" Montgomery, like some other outstanding commanders, had the same gift of being able to discern, amid the complications of a major conflict, the uncomplicated underlying reality. Hitler lacked this laser vision.

For it should have been evident to him, particularly after Alamein, Kursk, and the defeat of the Atlantic U-boats in the late spring of 1943, that he had indeed lost the initiative, that he was beginning to dance to the Allies' tune, and that unless he embarked on some constructive and radical rethinking, Nazi Germany, and all that it stood for, was doomed. Yet if Foch in 1943 had asked *"de quoi s'agit-il?"* he would surely have noted that the matter resolved itself in terms of two paramount facts: all possible strength must be concentrated on holding off Russia and preparing to meet the cross-Channel invasion which (now that American supplies and divisions could pour freely across the Atlantic) had become a certainty. To this end a Fortress Europe must be established on the most economically defensible scale, behind whose frontiers the concentrated German forces with their good inner communications might have some hope of resisting until the new terror weapon could be deployed, or Russia tired and sought a negotiated peace, or . . . well, something happened. Apart from this, everything was fundamentally irrelevant.

It is sometimes claimed that Hitler's "last ditch" mentality, as a military commander, derived from his experience of siege warfare in France and Flanders, with all that that implied of tenacious refusal to surrender ground—the mentality of the German infantryman who, particularly in 1916 and 1917, absorbed shock wave after shock wave of Allied attacks and so resolutely stood his ground. But this, surely, was no more than an intensification of a basic character trait. Hitler was the supreme possessive. He was the Reich and the Reich was Hitler: any extension of the Reich's territory (and his policy, as we have seen, was rapaciously expansionist) was an extension of himself. Any surrender of ground for those trivial reasons of tactics or strategy which the military theorists propounded was therefore unacceptable and, indeed, unimaginable, for it entailed the surrender of a part of Adolf Hitler.

Whatever the psychological origins of his mid-war policies may be, the results are indisputable. We have an image of Hitler lashing out blindly, reacting to the Allies' bait and failing, at the strategic level, to withdraw and concentrate his overextended forces so as to enable him to recover the initiative and himself strike again with effective strength. Considering his weakness on the critical Russian front, it was a grave miscalculation to pour troops and tanks of high quality into the Tunisian deathtrap and then, when the fight was clearly lost, to refuse Rommel's request to evacuate even skilled veterans and specialists. The Kesselschlacht, this time, destroyed his own army—and it was of his own creation.

Hitler subsequently justified his retention of the Tunisian foothold on the ground that it delayed the invasion of France by some six months. For the same spurious reason he made a case for his acceptance of Kesselring's argument in favor of confronting the Allies in the far south of Italy and stubbornly but slowly dragging a fiery rake up the whole peninsula, rather than Rommel's plan for a swift and calculated withdrawal to the line of the Alps—to the frontier, in fact, of a viable Fortress Germany. In each case he was mistaken. As to Tunisia and Torch, both Roosevelt and Churchill perceived that in late 1942 a cross-Channel invasion would be premature and thus there was nowhere else for their accumulating new divisions to get into the fight. What Hitler provided in Tunisia was, in effect, a theater where these raw troops (and their mainly inexperienced senior commanders) carried out a series of training exercises with live ammunition, a theater where Eisenhower could mature as a supreme commander and generals like Patton and Bradley could hone the skills that would ultimately be required in Normandy. As to Italy, Hitler never tumbled to the British strategy (so passionately advocated by Alanbrooke and so grudgingly accepted by the Americans), the strategy of seducing into Italy as many German divisions as possible from the vital regions of western Europe.

A contraction of the European perimeter undoubtedly involved risks. It was not simply a matter of continuing to prop up Mussolini, for the Duce was toppled in any case. But the surrender of the Foggia airfield complex to the Allies, the greater exposure of the armament industry in southern Germany to bombardment, the impairment or loss of the Ploesti oil reservoir, a halt to the flow of rare but essential metals from the Balkans and a greater threat to Mediterranean France were but a few of the daunting factors which had to be weighed. But the higher conduct of war is about priorities, about nice calculations of judgment, above all about realism. Hitler was incapable of applying the ancient philosophical principle of Occam's razor—of "cutting out the inessential." By endeavoring to retain everything, he lost everything. Like the Athenians who withdrew on to the Acropolis in the face of a Persian menace, he should have been prepared to sacrifice the desirable for the sake of the paramount. This, after all, was what the Russians had done, trading space for time. But he was too greedy.

The consequences of this self-indulgent dispersion of effort were plain to see on D-Day.

> At the beginning of 1944 Germany had over 300 divisions in the field, outside of the Reich. Of these, 179 were on the Russian front, 26 in the Balkan States, 22 in Italy, 53 in France and the Low Countries, 16 in Scandinavia and 8 in Finland. In various occupied countries 24 of these divisions were in process of formation. There was no general reserve in Germany. All Hitler's huge land forces were committed, and without denuding other fronts there could be no substantial increase of the Armies in the West.[2]

By June 6, 1944, that denudation had not occurred in any significant sense. The figures for the German Order of Battle in the west are: on April 4, 55 divisions, and on May 28, 58 divisions.

It may therefore be fairly asked whether by failing to answer the central and critical question *"de quoi s'agit-il?"* Hitler did not commit another of his major mistakes. Did the dissipation of over 50 divisions in southern Europe and another 24 on the northern flank make military sense at a time when, in Russia, German manpower was so deficient in the face of an inexhaustible enemy that frail Rumanian and Hungarian formations had to be thrust into the line: a time when, in Normandy, too many of the coastal defense divisions were second-rate? Suppose, for example, that the Americans on Omaha Beach, who only survived by a miracle the consequences of their own errors and of a stubborn resistance, had been met by those indomitable parachute units which uselessly poured away their blood at Cassino? Suppose Hitler had sensibly withdrawn a good proportion of his divisions from the perimeters of Europe and packed them into France. Would Churchill, always haunted by the Somme and Passchendaele, have then been prepared to allow the invasion to go ahead? At the very least a substantially stronger threat of opposition by the German army would have caused grave and possibly fatal dissension in the Allied council chambers. And—what always tends to be forgotten in later years—during the early phase of the Normandy fighting the issue was often in the balance. Who can estimate what the result might have been if even a few more hardened Wehrmacht or SS divisions had been readily available during, say, the first seven days?

HITLER'S MISTAKES

By the end of 1942, after the United States had entered the war, Germany's defeat was virtually unavoidable. But the ex-corporal who believed that "anyone can do the little job of directing operations in war" manifestly accelerated, by his egregious mistakes, that irreversible process.

9

ON THE TOBOGGAN

Down, down, down. Would the fall *never* come to an end?

—LEWIS CARROLL, *Alice's Adventures in Wonderland*

In a striking phrase, Mahatma Gandhi once observed of the British Empire that it was "on the toboggan." This was the condition of Hitler's Reich when, during the night of June 5, 1944, the first Allied airborne troops fell from the skies into Normandy.

The subsequent slide down the slope would certainly have been more gradual had it not been that arrangements for defense in the West were unnecessarily deficient in every important particular. Yet those fatal deficiencies can be traced, in each case, to miscalculations or other errors of judgment on the part of the Führer himself. In his Directive No. 32 of June 11, 1941, "Preparations for the period after Barbarossa," he had optimistically asserted that "After the destruction of the Soviet armed forces, Germany and Italy will be military masters of the European continent . . . No serious threat to Europe by land will then remain.'' By November 3, 1943, and his Directive No. 51, euphoria had modulated into ''The danger in the East remains, but a greater danger now appears in the West: an Anglo-Saxon landing! . . . I can, therefore, no longer take responsibility for further weakening in the West, in favour of other theatres of war.'' But this was mere rhetoric. Apart from bringing Rommel's furious and inventive energy to bear, too late, on the refurbishing of the Atlantic Wall, Hitler's response to the challenge which he himself had identified was desultory, inadequate and misconceived. Indeed, by keeping the number of his divisions in the West virtually static, at a time when Allied manpower and *matériel* in the British Isles were increasing to the point when it was said that only the barrage balloons kept those islands afloat, he was doing precisely what he had promised not to do—weakening the West, relatively, in favor of other theaters of war.

But the value of those divisions was further and critically impaired. To begin with, the command structure in the West (for which Hitler was wholly responsible) had a surrealist character. Theoretically von Rundstedt was the master, the deferential von Rundstedt, already 68, conservative in his conceptions and sluggish in his reactions. Yet because of Hitler's consistent policy of fragmentation, of ensuring that none of his subordinates possessed too much power, von Rundstedt had no compulsive authority over the SS divisions (which were Himmler's henchmen) or the parachute and antiaircraft formations (the latter, with their 88mm guns, so vital also in their antitank role), which looked to Göring. Guderian's position as inspector-general of Panzer troops blurred the lines of control over all the armored and motorized units. Worst of all, Hitler, as commander-in-chief and manipulator of OKW, exercised a ruthlessly idiosyncratic dominion over every aspect of operations, administrative, strategic and tactical. Even the reserves on which Rundstedt might expect to draw were in the clutch of others—lodged in Fromm's Reserve Army or, in the case of the Panzer training units, the lieges of Guderian. And even his rear areas were not under von Rundstedt's thumb, for the military governors, von Stülpnagel in Paris and von Falkenhausen in Belgium, exercised their own *droits de seigneur,* while Himmler and even von Ribbentrop, in varying degrees, had overt or less clearly defined prerogatives. Convenient though this kaleidoscope might be for Hitler's private purpose, it was unmanageable in the conditions of active warfare.

As might be expected, the contradictions inherent in the system were nakedly revealed at the crucial point: during the hours immediately following the Allied landings when, if it was to succeed, the center of gravity of the German counterthrust must be accurately, swiftly and massively responsive. But after a passionate debate about the proper use of the Panzers in Normandy, between Rommel on the one hand (who at Army Group B would have to fight the battle of the beaches, and wanted his armor close to the front) and, on the other hand, von Rundstedt, Guderian and Gehr von Schweppenburg (commander of Panzer Group West), who wished to hold back the armor inland, Hitler made another of his fatal and self-centered compromises. Four armored divisions would be grouped as an OKW reserve, but stationed miles away from the coast. They were, moreover, *only* to be employed as and when he himself might direct.

The result was disastrous. After the initial landings there were painful and, indeed, incredible delays before Hitler could be roused and persuaded to accept Rommel's plea for Panzer support. In consequence the two best armored divisions in the West, 12 SS and Panzer Lehr, were neutralized. In their crawl to the front both took such punishment from bombing that Panzer Lehr was unable to attempt an attack until June 9, and 12 SS impotently ran out of fuel. It was a classic example of what can go wrong when operations are tightly controlled from a far-distant headquarters, in complete ignorance of the relevant conditions at the front: a classic example, in fact, of the fatuity of Hitler's methods.

Apart from the armor, the divisions at Rommel's disposal were often of poor quality because of another of Hitler's characteristic aberrations, which had frequently led him astray in Russia. This was his naïve belief that if he nominated a new division, transferred a few troops to it from a cadre and stuck another pin in his map, that division existed in full fighting strength and could be counted on as such when he calculated his Order of Battle. But some of the "fortress divisions" were empty shells, fleshed out with the aging and convalescent, and lacking both transport and a respectable armament. "The infantry divisions contained numbers of Russians, Hungarians, Poles, Yugoslavs, Czechs, Romanians and Dutch, to name but a few of the nationalities in German service. Pay books were issued in eight different languages just to deal with the various peoples from the Soviet Union, of whom there were 60,000 in France."[1] Reinforcements were sometimes equally feeble. Rundstedt, whose tongue had a sharp edge, put it like this: "Often I would be informed that a new division was to arrive in France direct from Russia, or Norway, or central Germany. When it finally made its appearance in the west it would consist, all in all, of a divisional commander, a medical officer, and five bakers."

The story of the collapse in Normandy is so well known that it is only necessary to point to the two gross errors on Hitler's part which ensured that catastrophe was unavoidable. First there was the repetition of his "stand fast" syndrome, which had doomed so many of his soldiers to death or captivity in Tunisia, Italy and Russia. Once the Allies had landed in strength and consolidated their bridgehead (covered as it was with air forces against which the Luftwaffe could do no more than nibble, in spite of Göring's reckless promises in which his Führer had once again believed) nothing made military sense but to retire eastward as fast as possible behind the protective line of the Seine. Rommel saw this almost immediately. Von Rundstedt saw it. Even the "loyal" von Kluge, who replaced Rundstedt with high hopes of repelling the enemy, soon recognized the truth. Only Hitler remained stubbornly blind, and only Hitler could give the order to withdraw. The charnel house in the Falaise gap was the consequence.

The final attempt to break through to the sea in a massive *Panzer* drive via Mortain and Avranches, a purely Hitlerian conception, is another prime example of grandiose futility. The fact that at Bletchley Park all the relevant signals relating to the offensive were deciphered, so that General Bradley, forewarned, was able to trap the Germans in a carefully prepared bag offers no mitigation. Even if that cryptanalytical coup had not occurred, there was no possibility that the offensive could have more than a spoiling effect, no conceivable manner in which it could recover fortunes already lost. Instead, Hitler frittered away those remaining tanks and troops whose presence would have been invaluable during the retreat to Germany, which inevitably followed once Eisenhower had a grip on the northern shores of France. Precious blood had been poured down the drain.

It has been calculated that during the summer and autumn of 1944 the German army suffered more casualties than during the whole of the war up to the beginning of 1943—including the opening phase of Barbarossa and Stalingrad. Twenty-nine divisions were lost in the west; in the east ten had to be disbanded, as well as two in Italy and three in the Balkans. Blood was indeed being poured away at a tremendous rate. Between June and September there were 55,000 dead in the west and 340,000 missing; in the east the figures were far worse—215,000 dead and 627,000 missing. Yet in spite of the mistakes on Hitler's part which had accelerated this copious bloodletting, his armies in the west did their duty: that is to say, as the shattered units struggled back from France and the Low Countries toward Germany they were gradually knitted together and reinforced, so that as the year ran on a thin but unbroken gray line ensured that the war would continue into 1945. Any objective historian must applaud this as an extraordinary military achievement.

Hitler's contribution to the defensive withdrawal was largely hortatory. He understood and could devise the aggressive act, but the subtle maneuvers necessary for the extrication of defeated armies were foreign to his nature and beyond his comprehension. His despised generals did the professional job. Hitler's instinctive response to the crisis, as on similar occasions in Russia, was to scream. In the signals deciphered at Bletchley Park during this period there were numerous examples of the Führer in his declamatory mood. It is true that at the end of July he gave Göring (for what that was worth) the task of overhauling the war effort and armed Goebbels with plenipotentiary powers.* A million or more men were raked out as reinforcements for the Wehrmacht, but they were often too young or too old, and the new Volksgrenadier-Divisionen which sprang into being, though they were decked out with names reflecting the glory of the Prussian past, were ineffective "warriors for the working day" compared with the dead into whose shoes they stepped. Perhaps Hitler's most positive achievement was to continue to back Albert Speer in his astonishing regeneration of the German armaments industry, but at a time when the Russian air force was dominant from the Baltic to Romania and the Anglo-American combination controlled the skies of western Europe by day and, increasingly, by night, there was little that Hitler's exhortations or Speer's ingenuity could do to restore that air superiority over the battlefield which had become essential for victory. Most of the best pilots were dead anyway, and there was not enough fuel to train the newcomers adequately. All the cards seemed to be in the Allied hands. And few would have predicted, at the time, that they would play them so badly.

* Goebbels's appointment followed the July 20 plot and his full title was Reich Commissioner for Total Mobilization of Resources for War. But that cynical realist knew that it was too late, commenting to his aide that "If I had received these powers when I wanted them so badly" . . . in early 1943 . . . "victory would be in our pockets today and the war would probably be over. But it takes a bomb under his arse to make Hitler see reason."

Hitler (much encouraged by Goebbels) was constantly scanning the horizon for a Blücher who would bring salvation at this Waterloo. Both, in effect, were obsessed with the events of 1762 and "the Miracle of the House of Brandenburg." Both studied Carlyle's *Frederick the Great* intently, as if it were a prophetic book within which auguries of hope might be detected. In April, 1944, for example, Goebbels was visiting an army headquarters where he "developed his thesis that, for reasons of Historical Necessity and Justice, a change of fortune was inevitable, like the Miracle of the House of Brandenburg in the Seven Years' War. One of the staff officers had somewhat skeptically and ironically asked, 'What Czarina will die this time?' " However, on his return to Berlin Goebbels received the news of Roosevelt's death, immediately telephoned his late hosts to announce that "the Czarina *is* dead," and then rang Hitler on his private line. "My Führer I congratulate you! Roosevelt is dead. It is written in the stars that the second half of April will be the turning-point for us." Hitler was ecstatic. Both were, of course, wrong; but what is so revealing about Hitler's tendency to grasp at straws, and his inability to penetrate to the realities, is that while he was exalted by the death of the ailing Roosevelt (which barely affected the prosecution of the war) he never perceived that six months earlier he had actually been presented with a "Miracle of the House of Brandenburg" by the Allies themselves. For the German recovery after the Normandy campaign was indeed a miracle. And yet, in the final analysis, it was neither the stubborn resistance of his soldiers nor the Führer's exhortations which were responsible for that recovery so much as errors committed by the Anglo-American High Command.

The long and ultimately petulant disagreement between Eisenhower and Montgomery as to whether the Allies should advance toward Germany on a broad front or concentrate their resources for a single thrust in the north was a delaying distraction which, by preventing them from rapidly and forcefully exploiting the enemy's weakness, instead supplied a breathing space within which the German battleline could be re-formed. The failure to resolve this deadlock was a major failure of strategic imagination on the part of both the British and the Americans and an unpredictable bonus for Hitler. More particularly, the simultaneous failure to clear the seaward approaches to Antwerp immediately after the port itself was seized during the breakout from Normandy had many damaging consequences. It meant that most of the millions of tons of supplies on which Eisenhower's armies daily depended had to be hauled by road, cumbrously and slowly, from small harbors and beachheads far to the west. This in itself imposed a brake on further aggressive advances, a limitation painfully emphasized when, in Operation Market Garden, an abortive attempt was made to seize the Rhine crossings at Arnhem. For this occurred in September, yet it was not until November, after a conflict in blood and mud which recalled Passchendaele, that the banks of the Scheldt were seized, the waterways cleared and the first merchant ships docked in Antwerp. Thus, even had Arnhem succeeded, it is very difficult to see how the Allies could have maintained momentum by feeding and fostering a truly powerful thrust into the heart of Germany. All these errors, compounded, worked cumulatively in Hitler's favor, but there is little evidence that he read accurately the false conceptions in his opponents' minds: still less that he realized that the very errors which were keeping defeat from his door derived from a dogmatic belief, on the part of Eisenhower, Montgomery and the bulk of their generals (but *not* of Churchill), that the Germans were already on the run and that victory would be consummated by Christmas.

There is a curious note in the record of Hitler's *Table Talk* for June 24, 1943. "To achieve great things," he says, "it is necessary to burn many of one's boats behind one—especially those which are laden with personal prejudices. Reason alone must have the last word." Yet in the conduct of military operations his procedure was precisely the opposite—irrational, holding-out-to-the-last, flawed conceptually and in execution because its pattern was shaped by the flaws in his own personality. Reason, except in the form of some distorted logic based on false premises, rarely entered into his equations. And so it was that as a meaningful defense of Germany's western frontiers began to seem not impossible during the autumn months of 1944, Hitler did not fervently concentrate everything on consolidating those defenses but, in the only way he understood, set up another Blitz. Aggression at all costs, aggression preferably shrouded by deceit and launched unexpectedly, was his favorite and characteristic mode—in Poland, in Norway, in France in 1940, in Barbarossa, in the Mortain offensive in Normandy. Now it became the basis for his last major offensive in the west—the Ardennes. It is a measure of his generalship that within a month he lost 120,000 soldiers, 600 tanks and assault guns, and over 1,600 aircraft—and achieved nothing. He might console himself by quoting, as he did, a letter written by his idol Frederick the Great in 1760: "I started this war with the most wonderful army in Europe; today I've got a muck heap. I have no leaders any more, my generals are incompetent, the troops are wretched." But the truth was that it was he, and he alone, who had wrecked the "wonderful" Wehrmacht: it was he who, by the draconian measures and murders which followed the July 20 plot, had virtually extinguished the last spark of initiative and imagination in the minds of his subordinates: and it was Hitler, and Hitler alone, who devised and supervised down to the last petty detail the venture which was later canonized as the Battle of the Bulge. "The implacable resentment with which his enemies pursued him," wrote Lord Macaulay of King Frederick, "though originally provoked by his own unprincipled ambition, excited in him a thirst for vengeance which he did not even attempt to conceal." Such was Hitler's reaction: the muck heap had failed him in Normandy, V weapons were a diminishing asset, the attempt on his life had revealed layer upon layer of treachery in every area of the Reich, civil as well as military. So! His response must be another thunderbolt.

He began thinking on these lines even before the end of the Normandy battle. As early as August 19 Jodl noted in his diary: "The *Führer* discussed the equipment and manpower position in the West with the Chief of OKW, Chief of Army Staff and Speer. *Prepare to take the offensive in November* when the enemy air forces can't operate." And then, on September 16, he told Guderian, Keitel and Jodl that his ideas had now clarified. He had the solution. "I have just made a momentous decision. I shall go over to the counter-attack, that is to say out of the Ardennes with the objective—Antwerp." The date is significant. It was the day *before* the Allied airborne drop at Arnhem (which took the Germans completely by surprise). The Ardennes offensive was not, therefore, a mere reflex tit-for-tat: it was the maturation of long and thoughtful planning.

All the generals were appalled. Model said, "This plan hasn't got a leg to stand on." But though what were called "smaller solutions" were ventilated, they were brushed aside and on November 1 Jodl issued Hitler's final order for a crossing of the Meuse and a drive for Antwerp by two *Panzer* armies, endorsed in the Führer's own hand with the menacing rubric *Nicht abändern,* "no alterations permitted." After that (and after July 20) no one with a concern for his neck was going to propose alterations.

On paper the plan made strategic sense and it seemed as though Hitler had correctly identified, in Antwerp, the Allies' Achilles' heel. He summarized it as follows:

> The Netherlands are to be retained; not an inch of German territory is to be abandoned; the Allies are to be prevented from using Antwerp and

> resistance is therefore to be kept up as long as possible at the mouth of the Scheldt; the Allied air bases are to be held as far as possible from the heart of Germany, and the Ruhr and the Saar are to be protected.

Moreover, the military virtues of the basic idea have been acclaimed by a number of able critics, including Sir Basil Liddell Hart, who wrote in his *History of the Second World War* that "The idea, the decision and the strategic plan were entirely Hitler's own. It was a brilliant concept and might have proved a brilliant success *if* he had still possessed sufficient resources, as well as forces, to ensure it a reasonable chance of succeeding in its big aims." But it was precisely those forces and resources that Hitler now lacked, and precisely why von Rundstedt, who privately washed his hands of the whole business, was later caused such pain, and such professional chagrin, when the operation came to be christened the "Rundstedt Offensive."

For this interpretation misses the point. Antwerp was indeed named as the objective, but Antwerp was never Hitler's prime target and it is in this respect that, once again, he made a politico-military misjudgment. Two major premises conditioned his thinking. The first was purely military: if he could drive a solid wedge between the British and American armies, this must throw them into irrecoverable confusion. (His deeply founded contempt for the morale of the American soldier had not diminished). But there was another consideration, optimistically political. When Himmler addressed an assembly of Gauleiters at Possen on August 3, the voice was that of the SS Reichsminister who had been appointed Commander-in-Chief of the Home Army after the July plot, but the thoughts were the thoughts of his Führer. "When weariness is gaining a hold on the other side, then will come the time to talk of peace. A new army, fully ready to fight, will give the Führer the arguments and the triumphs which will allow him to dictate the peace." In other words a debacle at Antwerp ought not only to castrate the Allies' military strength: it might be expected to shatter their will, cause them to despair of achieving their war aims, induce a split with the Russians and, if all went well, be consummated by a negotiated peace. It is not necessary to rehearse all the clinching evidence available to demonstrate that by the end of 1944 any hope of demolishing the overwhelming military power of the Anglo-Americans, or of expecting that they could be terrified into abandoning their policy of unconditional surrender, was grotesque, and should have been seen to be grotesque. Once again Hilter had concocted a chimera, in a command post situated, as it were, in Cloudcuckooland.

And once it was all over, once the Mark IVs and the Tigers of two *Panzer* armies had creaked back to safety through the mists, the mud and the snow of the Ardennes valleys, the scoresheet showed that the German achievement was indeed null and void. Two *Panzer* (and one infantry) armies attacking, on a front of fifty miles, one armored and four infantry divisions without defenses in depth or any immediate reserves, had failed to reach, let alone cross, the Meuse. Certainly the Americans had lost 1,000 tanks and many thousands of vehicles. They had fired over 1,000,000 rounds of artillery ammunition and enormous quantities from their small arms. But the logistic resilience of the Americans was so great that most of these losses were made up within *two weeks*. More to the point is the fact that while Hitler and OKW were preoccupied with the Ardennes operation the Russians were able, in January, to launch successfully their massive New Year offensive across the Upper Vistula, so that at Yalta in early February Stalin could announce from a position of great authority that within three weeks Warsaw had fallen, Budapest was besieged and his forces were now within forty miles of Berlin. Far from shattering the military or political cohesion of the Grand Alliance, Hitler had enabled it to obtain in strategic harmony a major victory on two far-distant fronts. The possibility dreaded by the old German General Staff long before 1914 had now been realized.

Indeed, if Hitler had been capable of reflection he would have noted that during the course of the battle something symbolic had occurred. The spearhead of one of his divisions had actually caught a glimpse of the Meuse! So it had been outside Moscow, late in 1941, when another spearhead unit observed on the skyline the unattainable Kremlin. Then again, in the later thrust down into the Caucasus, some agile soldiery had clambered to the summit of Mount Elbruz, planted a flag there, and looked out over the Promised Land they were never to enter. This, Hitler might have reckoned, was the paradigm of his career as Führer and warlord: always the promise, but never the final, clinching performance. We think back to the City of Mahagonny, that image deployed in Chapter Two: the city of nets, "but in the net nothing has been caught."

But Hitler's mood in early 1945 was not one of reflection. On the contrary, it was more than usually sullen, vicious, vindictive and intemperate. He was now like a Roman emperor hag-ridden by doubts even about the Praetorian Guard. The sad story of the Sixth SS Panzer Army provides a perfect illustration. Commanded by that rough but able *condottiere* Sepp Dietrich, it had been given on the Führer's insistence a special and, as many experts felt and feel, an ill-judged role in the Ardennes offensive. Soon afterward Hitler had the notion that as the Russians were committed with 180 divisions up on the Vistula front, there might be some profit in attacking and perhaps even turning their southern flank in Hungary. Off to the shores of Lake Balaton, therefore, he whisked the Sixth SS Panzer Army, thus removing from the West the main mobile force which might have been held in reserve to counterattack the Anglo-Americans once they crossed the Rhine into Germany.

The result is vividly summarized by one of the footnotes in Hugh Trevor-Roper's *The Last Days of Hitler:*

> The *Leibstandarte Adolf Hitler* was a division of the *Waffen SS,* and at this time was fighting on the Upper Danube with the Sixth SS *Panzer* Army, under the command of Hitler's gangster-favourite Sepp Dietrich. The LAH was ordered to attack according to Hitler's strategical plans, but owing to an error in the weather forecast the attack was timed to take place on a day of torrential rain. Hitler's plan was nevertheless regarded as sacred; the attack was made; and a disastrous massacre was the consequence. When this failure was reported to Hitler, he was furious with the LAH, and ordered them to remove their armbands as a punishment. The indignant soldiers tore off their orders and decorations, and sent them to Hitler, through Himmler, in a tin chamber-pot. They also sent the arm, complete with armband, of one of their dead comrades.[2]

"Things fall apart," as the poet W. B. Yeats wrote, "the centre cannot hold." And the difficulty was that the man at the center was now approaching the condition of a burned-out case.

For if a collage were to be pieced together from the innumerable eyewitness descriptions which are now available of Hitler during the last five months of his life, a picture would emerge whose distortions of normality, though strictly representational, would make it worthy of a Braque or a Picasso. The body is warped and ungainly: the uniform, once almost prim, is slovenly and ill-kempt. Whether or not Parkinson's disease has supervened, the hands are so tremulous that others must inscribe documents requiring the Führer's signature. (Hitler himself was well aware of this revealing incapacity. When he presented Speer with a signed photograph in March, 1945, he confessed: "Lately it's been hard for me to write even a few words in my own hand. You know how it shakes. Often I can hardly complete my signature. What I've written for you came out almost illegible.") The dull luster of the eyes is that of a dying fish. The voice whose *timbre* intoxicated the Nuremberg rallies and, even on radio, sent shivers through the western world is now hoarse, feeble, and sometimes almost inaudible. Old companions from the triumphant past note his emaciation, his pallor, his bloated cheeks: soine vital spark seems to have been quenched. It is true that even now the fury which, like a malignant fever, constantly consumes him allows an occasional break in the clouds that blur his mind, for records exist from those who remember witnessing a passing recovery of clarity and authority: then they still felt themselves to be in the presence of a man who could miraculously save Germany. But these impressions were exceptional, and no doubt they were sometimes based on wishful thinking or composed later to perpetuate a legend. In any case their testimony is belied by a mass of contradictory evidence. The truth is that we are observing a man in the late stages of pathological decrepitude, whose mental ability to construct rational combinations is already approaching a terminal condition.

In fact it may be argued that from early 1945 onward, though certainly no precise date can be fixed, there is no longer any point in attempting to analyze Hitler's "mistakes." At the least, a mistake implies an error which has resulted from some sort of calculated choice between possible options. However ill-founded the logic involved in that choice, a kind of logic is discernible. Until he took the decision to launch the Ardennes offensive it may be plausibly maintained that the majority of Hitler's actions and *Diktats,* whether political or military, had been preceded by some such form of thought process, occasionally prolonged and not infrequently identifiable. Misguided though it was, the Ardennes concept itself had a sufficiently rational quality for some, as has been seen, to have dared to describe it as brilliant. But between the Battle of the Bulge and his death few of Hitler's actions can be justified as those of a man who is even marginally in command of his faculties.

In certain English medieval Churches it is still possible to study and admire the remnants of those elaborate wall paintings which, in the early days, uplifted and instructed a devoted congregation. Amid the normal biblical typology, there may sometimes be observed the relics of a very different drama. Battle scenes, usually forbidden to the artist, are in progress. Spears are brandished, chargers rear, casualties tumble.

The presentation is that of the *psychomachia,* the spiritual struggle between Good and Evil. Though good was scarcely the quality that had striven, throughout his life, to dominate the force of evil in Hitler's nature, one could still maintain that in his case, too, there had occurred over the decades a private *psychomachia:* a contest in which the dark and dreadful side of his personality had been challenged, and often checked, by intellectual powers which cannot be denied him and to which some of his most successful coups can be traced. Now, in 1945, his waning mental strength had virtually abandoned the field, leaving him to the sway of all that was most loathsome in his makeup, the inhumanity, the egocentricity, the nihilism, the vicious contempt for the very German people whose overlordship he had claimed as his right. We can hardly ascribe "mistakes" to a psychiatric catastrophe.

The direct military consequences of this inner disintegration were acutely recorded in his memoirs, *Inside Hitler's Headquarters, 1939–1945*, by General Walther Warlimont: "The determination of one man possessed of the devil governed everything; the machinery of command churned out orders in normal form though there might be no one to receive them . . . Hitler's leadership was now without object or objective, but the last crazy orders continued to issue forth stamped with his own faults and his own phraseology."

Nowhere was the savagery that had now become relentless displayed more nakedly than in the treatment of his commanders who, like Roman legionaries striving to stem the barbarian tide, still did their professional utmost to shore up the ruins of front lines which the Führer himself never visited. To "fail" as a general had of course been, over the years, an increasingly suicidal dereliction. But now Hitler's reaction was usually automatic: "off with his head." The men in charge of doomed cities in the forward areas, particularly on the Russian front, must always have heard with sinking hearts that a Führer decree had elevated the city's status (on paper) to that of a fortress: their options in defending the indefensible were then either to fight to the death, to retreat, or to surrender. Either of the last two choices meant execution, or, at best, dishonor and dismissal. The fate of those who allowed the Americans to snatch a crossing of the Rhine at Remagen was not easily forgotten: it was christened, in fact, "the shock of Remagen" and Speer recalled that it "kept many of the responsible men in a state of terror until the end of the war."

In any case, the old guard had vanished, many in the abattoir which followed the assassination failure of July 20: Rundstedt, Rommel,

Kluge, Manstein, Halder, even the pliable Zeitzler, who was both ejected and robbed of the right to wear a uniform. Model, that supreme defender of the last ditch, committed suicide in the Ruhr once the Allies had closed their pincers around it. Guderian and Kesselring remained as impotent survivors, but in the main the marshals now available for the Napoleon who lurked in his Berlin bunker were second-raters. Who, in the great victorious days, would have put his money on Ferdinand Schoerner, "the Bloodhound," "the People's General"? Yet, after service as chief of the National Socialist Political Guidance Staff of the Armed Forces in 1944, he was promoted by Hitler to the rank of general field-marshal and expected to withstand, on the Silesian front, the Russians' final and implacable advance into Berlin. Men of straw led phantom divisions, yet from his command post Hitler optimistically moved them around as though this was the inspired and efficient Wehrmacht of 1940.

The situation of the Luftwaffe was no less parlous. Its father figure, Field-Marshal Milch, was eradicated in January, 1945. (Udet and Jeschonnek had, of course, already committed suicide.) His successor as secretary of state for air, Koller, was a desk administrator who lacked the nerve to stand up to Göring and Hitler. In any case, the real disease of the Luftwaffe was a broken heart. Incompetence on high, inadequate equipment, and above all unmerited slurs on their courage had eroded the morale of the few experienced pilots who still survived. A study prepared for the historical division of the U.S. Army records the efforts of "the group of former commanders who in January, 1945, had sought from Generaloberst von Greim and General Koller permission personally to inform the supreme commander of the Wehrmacht of the bitterness of their troops at Göring's unfair charges that they lacked fighting spirit and to present to him proposals regarding a more appropriate use of the Jagdwaffe. The attempt, however, had ended with Göring himself receiving a delegation of fighter commanders led by Oberst Lutzow, listening to what they had to say, and terminating the discussion by calling their action 'mutiny' and threatening to have Oberst Lutzow shot." [3]

Hitler was perfectly aware of Göring's deficiencies, though for "political" reasons which in the circumstances are difficult to comprehend he refused to dispose of him. And he, too, had lost faith in his pilots. "Göring," Guderian heard him shout, "your Luftwaffe isn't worth a damn! It doesn't deserve to be an independent branch of service any more. And that's your fault. You're lazy!" But the guilt was largely

Hitler's. Apart from buttressing Göring, he had interfered with the technical development of his air force at every stage, insisting either on the wrong machines, or the wrong deployment, or the wrong tactics, or the wrong leaders. It was Hitler who had destroyed the last hope of the Luftwaffe, its unmatched jet fighters, by ordering that they should be diverted to bombing operations. One of the finest pilots of those aircraft was Johannes Steinhoff, who had an indisputable record of battle service in the West, in the Mediterranean and on the Russian front. Though his face was incinerated when his jet crashed on takeoff, he won another battle, with himself, to become a chairman of NATO's military command and to write *The Last Chance,* in which with bitter and burning words he describes his share in the revolt of his disillusioned peers and the shambles to which Göring had reduced a superb weapon of war, the Luftwaffe. In the end it was not even a weapon. By the month of the final surrender, its rate of effort against the Russians was no more than fifty sorties a day! "The responsibility," as Matthew Cooper has summed it up in his history of the Luftwaffe, "lies not with the men and officers of the German Air Force, whose exploits during the war can only claim respect, it lies with the Luftwaffe high command, whose mode of operation disgraced its profession of arms, and, above all, with Hitler, Führer and Supreme Commander. It was the actions of this War Lord, one totally unworthy of the title, that brought the Luftwaffe to defeat as surely as night follows day and, with it, the downfall of the Third Reich."[4]

But the defeat of his Reich was now precisely what Hitler had in mind—an inglorious Samson, determined to bring down the pillars of the temple in chaos around him. The absolute quality of his "scorched-earth" policy for Germany during the last few months of his regime is the supreme example of how nihilism and egomania, always so prominent in his personality, had finally triumphed, leaving no leeway for statesmanship or rational considerations. Germany had failed *him*! He faced defeat. Therefore Germany, like his generals, must pay the extreme penalty. His notorious affirmation to Speer puts the matter plainly: "If the war is lost, the people will be lost also. It is not necessary to worry about what the German people will need for elemental survival. On the contrary, it is best for us to destroy even these things. For the nation has proved to be the weaker, and the future belongs solely to the stronger eastern nation. In any case only those who are inferior will remain after this struggle, for the good have already been killed."

The danger signals shone brightly even before the Allied failure at Arnhem had offered some hope of a prolonged resistance. By the late summer of 1944 Hitler's plans had already been elaborated in fine detail. Nothing was to be left for the advancing Allies; no industries, no basic services like gas, water or electricity, no communications system. In the registries all personal files were to be destroyed. Theaters and opera houses, castles and churches were to be razed. On September 7, 1944, an editorial in the *Völkischer Beobachter,* inserted by order of the Führer, summarized his requirements and, in effect, informed his people that what not even the Russians or the Anglo-American bombers had achieved, he would demand from them—a total sacrifice of their way of life: "Not a German stalk of wheat is to feed the enemy, not a German mouth to give him information, not a German hand to offer him help. He is to find every foot-bridge destroyed, every road blocked—nothing but death, annihilation and hatred will meet him." Hitler's thoughts in Goebbels' prose.

The memoirs of Albert Speer are those of a haunted man, and the reader is himself haunted at times by the suspicion that in this confessional the author, whether consciously or unconsciously, has reconstituted the true situation in order to authenticate an *apologia pro vita sua*. Nevertheless there is no doubt, as was recorded at Nuremberg, that Hitler's "scorched-earth" policy went along the lines described so vividly by Speer in his reminiscences, or that Speer himself put his life at risk in endeavoring to thwart it. That Speer's efforts were directed mainly at preserving Germany's industrial infrastructure may be ascribed to higher motives, or merely to the anguish of a brilliant technocrat who could not bear to stand by and watch the destruction of what he had so largely created. But in this respect his case rests: the plan was there, and he undermined it, thus making to his own countrymen at least some repayment for the years during which he had assisted Hitler without compunction or reservations. Posterity will probably judge him to be the least contemptible of the Führer's lackeys, sensitive, percipient, intellectual and, in the end, self-aware and self-flagellant—even though neither his sensitivity nor his percipience prevented him, for example, from endorsing and even encouraging the massive use of slave labor. As Hitler's ideas about the destruction of Germany hardened and became explicit during the nerve-racked spring of 1945, in directive after directive, Speer made his *gran rifiuto*, the disciple rejecting the master.

That such a man should have turned against Hitler at the time of his greatest need, and for such reasons—even to the length of an abortive plan to suffocate him in his bunker—is a telling example of how Hitler had lost all credibility and now, a monster revealed, could command no more loyalty from even the most faithful and grateful of his lieutenants. For in a sense, his destructive intent was more monstrous than the Holocaust and more merciless than his designs on Russia: it was aimed at his own people, his *Volk,* the sheep who had so blindly followed his lead. But it is not to be regarded as a "mistake." It was the uninhibited expression of his true personality. "His seizures of violence could come upon him all the more strongly because there were no human emotions in him to oppose them. He simply could not let anyone approach his inner being because that core was lifeless, empty."

What should be the epitaph of such a man? It is to be found, appropriately enough, in Dr. Johnson's *The Vanity of Human Wishes:*

> He left the name, at which the world grew pale,
> To point a moral, or adorn a tale.

NOTES

Chapter One

1. Alan Bullock, *Hitler, a Study in Tyranny.*
2. A passionate account is in Johannes Steinhoff, *The Last Chance.*
3. Hugh Trevor-Roper, *The Last Days of Hitler,* 2nd Ed., p. 131.
4. Albert Speer, *Inside the Third Reich,* p. 471.
5. Trevor-Roper, introduction to *Hitler's Table Talk.*
6. Svetlana Alliluyeva, *Letters to a Friend.*

Chapter Two

1. "Germinal," by A. E. The preceding lines are also relevant: "In ancient shadows and twilights Where childhood had strayed, The world's great sorrows were born And its heroes made."
2. Speer, *op. cit.,* p. 181.
3. Trevor-Roper, *op. cit.,* p. 69.
4. A useful summary of the prewar plots is in Peter Hoffman, *The History of the German Resistance 1933–1945.*
5. Norman Stone, review in *The Times Literary Supplement.*
6. Speer, *op. cit.,* p. 298.

Chapter Three

1. Gordon A. Craig, *Germany,* p. 633.
2. Craig, *op. cit.*
3. Figures from Martin Gilbert, *Atlas of the Holocaust.*
4. The names in this section are selected from the Appendix, "300 Notable Émigrés," in Fleming and Bailyn, *The Intellectual Migration, Europe and America.*
5. Szilard's substantial autobiographical memoir, pp. 94–151 in Fleming and Bailyn, *op. cit.,* provides both a particularly vivid picture of the emigratory process and of the solidarity of the academic community. It also shows how at this time his mind was buzzing with new ideas about atomic energy.

Chapter Four

1. Bullock, *op. cit.*
2. Bullock, *op. cit.*
3. Quoted in Gordon A. Craig, *Germany 1866–1945*, p. 590.
4. Craig, *op. cit.*, p. 595.
5. For a severe analysis of Riefenstahl's cinematic propaganda, see Susan Sontag, *Fascinating Fascism*, in her *Under the Sign of Saturn* (New York: Farrar, Straus and Giroux, 1980).

Chapter Five

1. In a review in *The Times Literary Supplement*.
2. Terence Prittie, *Germans against Hitler*, p. 108.

Chapter Six

1. Major-General Walter Dornberger, *V2*, p. 187.

Chapter Seven

1. Quoted in David Irving, *The Rise and Fall of the Luftwaffe*.
2. Matthew Cooper, *The German Army 1933–1945*, p. 209.
3. Albert Seaton, *The German Army 1933–1945*, p. 166.
4. Seaton, *op. cit.*, p. 179.
5. General Guderian, *Panzer Leader*, p. 194.

Chapter Eight

1. Cooper, *op. cit.*
2. L. F. Ellis, *Victory in the West*, Vol. 1 (British Official Series).

Chapter Nine

1. Cooper, *op. cit.*, p. 496.
2. Trevor-Roper, *op. cit.*, p. 100.
3. Steinhoff, *op. cit.*, p. 130.
4. Matthew Cooper, *The German Air Force 1933–1945*, p. 378.

BIBLIOGRAPHY

I have consulted *passim* the relevant volumes in the British official series of histories of the Second World War. Some of the other books from which I have derived insight or information are:

Balfour, Michael. *Propaganda in War 1939–1945*. Routledge and Kegan Paul, 1979.

Bennett, Ralph. *Ultra in the West*. Hutchinson, 1979.

Bonhoeffer, Dietrich. *No Rusty Swords*. Collins, 1965.

Bormann, Martin. *The Bormann Letters*. Weidenfeld and Nicolson, 1954.

Broszat, Martin. *The Hitler State*. Longman, 1981.

Bullock, Alan. *Hitler*. Odhams Press, 1952.

Calvocoressi, Peter, and Guy Wint. *Total War*. Allen Lane, 1972.

Carver, Field Marshal Lord (ed.). *The War Lords*. Weidenfeld and Nicolson, 1976.

Cecil, Robert. *Hitler's Decision to Invade Russia*. Davis-Poynter, 1975.

Churchill, W. S. *The Second World War*. 6 vols. Cassell.

Cooper, Martin. *The German Army 1933–1945*. Macdonald and Jane's, 1978; *The German Air Force 1933–1945*. Jane's, 1981.

Craig, Gordon A. *Germany 1866–1945*. Oxford University Press, 1978.

Doenitz, Grand Admiral Karl. *Memories*. Weidenfeld and Nicolson, 1959.

Dornberger, Major-General Walter. *V2*. Hurst and Blackett, 1952.

Erickson, John. *The Road to Stalingrad*. Weidenfeld and Nicolson, 1975.

Fleming, Donald, and Bernard Bailyn (eds.). *The Intellectual Migration, Europe and America, 1930–1961*. Harvard University Press, 1969.

Foot, M.R.D. *Resistance*. Eyre Methuen, 1976.

Fraser, General David. *Alanbrooke*. Collins, 1982.

Frischauer, Willi. *Himmler*. Odhams Press, 1953.

Gilbert, Martin. *Winston Churchill, Vol. V, 1922–1939*. Heinemann, 1976; *Auschwitz and the Allies,* Michael Joseph/Rainbird, 1984; *Atlas of the Holocaust,* Michael Joseph, 1982.

Gisevius, Hans Berndt. *To the Bitter End*. Cape, 1948.
Goebbels, Joseph. *The Goebbels Diaries*. Secker and Warburg, 1978.
Görlitz, Walter. *The German General Staff*. Hollis and Carter, 1953.
Gowing, Margaret. *Britain and Atomic Energy 1939–1945*. Macmillan, 1964.
Haffner, Sebastian. *The Meaning of Hitler*. Weidenfeld and Nicolson, 1979.
Henry, Clarisse and Marc Hillel. *Children of the SS*. Hutchinson, 1976.
Herwarth, Johnnie von. *Against Two Evils*. Collins, 1981.
Hinsley, F. H. *et al.* (eds.). *British Intelligence in the Second World War*, Vol. I (1979), Vol. II (1981). Her Majesty's Stationery Office.
Hitler, Adolf. *Mein Kampf*. Hutchinson, 1969; *Hitler's Table Talk*, Weidenfeld and Nicolson, 1953.
Hoffman, Peter. *The History of the German Resistance 1933–1945*. Macdonald and Jane's, 1977.
Irving, David. *The Mare's Nest*. Kimber, 1964; *The Virus House*, Kimber, 1967; *The Rise and Fall of the Luftwaffe*, Weidenfeld and Nicolson, 1974; *The War Path*, Michael Joseph, 1978; *Hitler's War*, Hodder and Stoughton, 1977.
Jäckel, Eberhard. *Hitler's World View*. Harvard University Press, 1981.
John, Otto. *Twice Through the Lines*. Macmillan, 1969.
Jones, R. V. *Most Secret War: British Scientific Intelligence 1939–1945*. Hamish Hamilton, 1978.
Laqueur, Walter. *The Terrible Secret*. Weidenfeld and Nicolson, 1980.
Liddell Hart, Sir Basil. *History of the Second World War*. Cassell, 1970 (ed.); *The Rommel Papers*, Collins, 1953.
Macksey, Kenneth. *Guderian*. Macdonald and Jane's, 1975; *Kesselring*, Batsford, 1978.
Masterman, J. C. *The Double-Cross System*. Yale University Press, 1972.
Namier, Sir Lewis. *In the Nazi Era*. Macmillan, 1952.
O'Neill, Robert J. *The German Army and the Nazi Party*. Cassell, 1966.
Prittie, Terence. *Germans against Hitler*. Hutchinson, 1964.
Reitlinger, Gerald. *The Final Solution*. Vallentine Mitchell, 1953; *The SS: Alibi of a Nation*, Heinemann, 1956.
Ribbentrop, Joachim von. *The Ribbentrop Memoirs*. Weidenfeld and Nicolson, 1954.
Robertson, Esmonde M. (ed.). *The Origins of the Second World War*. Macmillan, 1971.
Seaton, Albert. *The Russo-German War*. Arthur Barker, 1971; *The Fall of Fortress Europe*, Batsford, 1981; *The German Army 1933–1945*, Weidenfeld and Nicolson, 1982.
Shirer, William. *The Rise and Fall of the Third Reich*. Secker and Warburg, 1959.

Speer, Albert. *Inside the Third Reich*. Weidenfeld and Nicolson, 1970; *Spandau: The Secret Diaries,* Weidenfeld and Nicolson, 1976; *Infiltration,* Weidenfeld and Nicolson, 1981.

Steinhoff, Johannes. *The Last Chance*. Hutchinson, 1977.

Stern, J. P. *Hitler: The Führer and the People*. Fontana, 1975.

Strawson, Major-General John. *Hitler as Military Commander*. Batsford, 1971.

Sydnor, Charles W., Jr. *Soldiers of Destruction: The SS Death's Head Division 1933–1945*. Princeton University Press, 1977.

Taylor, A.J.P. *The Origins of the Second World War*. Hamish Hamilton, 1961; *English History, 1914–1945,* Oxford University Press, 1965.

Trevor-Roper, Hugh. *The Last Days of Hitler*. 2nd ed., Macmillan, 1950.

Weinberg, Gerhard L. *World in Balance: Behind the Scenes of World War Two*. University Press of New England, 1981.

Wheeler-Bennett, J. W. *The Nemesis of Power*. Macmillan, 1953.

Winterbotham, Group Captain F. W. *The Nazi Connection*. Weidenfeld and Nicolson, 1978.

Wistrich, Robert. *Who's Who in Nazi Germany*. Weidenfeld and Nicolson, 1982.

INDEX

I